By Elyssa Nager

ISBN: 978-0-9908837-8-4

Disclaimer
Neither the author nor the publisher assumes any responsibility for errors, omissions or contrary interpretations of the subject matter herein. Any perceived slight of any individual or organization is purely unintentional. The information provided in this book is designed to provide helpful information on the subjects discussed. This book is designed to provide information and motivation to its readers. This book is not meant to be used, nor should it be used, to diagnose or treat a medical or mental health condition. For any diagnosis of any mental or medical health issue, consult your own physician or psychologist. The publisher and author are not responsible for any medical, mental, health or legal needs that may require medical, mental health supervision or support of legal counsel and are not liable for any damages or negative consequences from any ~~ment, action application or preparation to any per~~ this book. References are provided for infor~~ only and do not constitute an end~~ sites or other sources. Use of t' ~~ok is solely at your own risk. N ~~olisher shall be liable for any damages ~~ot limited to special, incidental, consequentia~ ~ damages. You are responsible for your own choices, actions and results.

Dedication

For all that choose AMAZING
regardless of what life throws at them.

Contents

Foreword   5

Introduction   9

Part 1: Living with fleas   15

  1.   Discarded...   17

  2.   About fleas (and crushing them!)   21

  3.   An answer to how emotional abuse works   27

  4.   The flea circus and why we stay   35

  5.   So, how do you know you've got fleas?
Clues and red flags   49

A personal aside: How freakin' naive can you be?   63

Part 2: A Bug-free life   69

Step 1:   You are all that you need   75

Step 2:   Exterminate the flea   81

Step 3:   Choose a flea-free haven   89

Step 4:   It's all about the we   95

Step 5:   Kick anxiety to the curb   103

Step 6:   Change the story   113

Step 7:   Practice mindfulness   125

Step 8:   Nutrition and exercise   143

Step 9:   Adopt reminder strategies   149

Step 10: Be weary of lawyers and the legal system   155

Step 11: Create boundaries   163

Step 12: Highly detailed parenting agreements   171

Step 13: Get your financial house in order   177

Step 14: Create you vision   185

Step 15: Dating   191

Step 16: Own Amazing!   197

Epilogue: Changing the way the world views emotional abuse   201

Resources   205

Foreword

Crushing Fleas by Elyssa Nager is a very important story. It is also an important contribution to the cannon of women's stories collected over the past sixty years as the voice of women strengthened and we understood the power of sharing our stories. We are not alone. Community is the cure. Breaking the silence dissolves the shame women so often feel when they try to stand up for themselves and fail—and also when they don't try. It empowers us and restores us. Together we can shift this severe imbalance in our culture known as the patriarchy but which harms men and boys and all genders as much as women.

When I first read Crushing Fleas I assumed there was abuse in Elyssa's childhood and that, as so often happens, she was repeating the pattern. We draw the patterns of our childhood to us until we are healed of buried trauma. But in this case Elyssa was not repeating a pattern. She appears to have been targeted and groomed. A naïve 'innocent abroad'. Pinocchio seduced to enter Candyland–but the lie was only to herself–that everything was OK, that all her instincts and intuitions were wrong. This was her dream come true, wasn't it?

There is a phrase, Droit du seigneur, which means the "right of the lord." Evidently, in medieval Europe feudal lords were allowed to have sexual relations with subordinate women on their wedding nights, prior to their grooms. As I read Crushing Fleas that phrase kept repeating in my mind. It seems this person, like so many men, felt he had the "right of the lord", in this case not referring to sex but to everything Elyssa owned and her own personal power. He seemed to have felt his wife was his subordinate. This is not a new story by any means. However, what her then husband achieved in appropriating Elyssa's wealth for himself and excluding her from that which she earned is deeply shocking and horrifying that it's legal anywhere.

Elyssa is now WOKE as we say and in a healthy relationship ready to educate women and awaken them to the minefields they may potentially encounter. She not only shares her personal story but generously provides a roadmap of very practical advice and recommendations for anyone who has already fallen into this trap and needs a guiding light.

We still live in a very oppressive culture. For example, women still earn 20%-25% less than men. It wasn't until the Equal Opportunity Credit Act of 1974 that made it unlawful for any creditor to discriminate against any applicant on the basis of race, color, religion, national origin, sex, or marital status that women were assured credit cards without a husband cosigning. Women are frequently still nervous about money. Elyssa left her then husband to the money management and in a legal and seemingly irreversible way was stripped of the assets she had earned.

Later, in recovery and unraveling the terrible ordeal she had been through, Elyssa had the courage to ask herself, How did I create this situation for myself? What was my role in it? This is the only way we stop being victims. Elyssa realized that she had ignored her intuition that something wasn't right. Also, that she wasn't educated in handling

money and handed the management over to her then partner. That, and by wanting the dream to stay intact and keep
everyone happy, another female trait we need to look at, she
abdicated responsibility. Her bravery in sharing those hard-
won insights and taking responsibility for her role is the
game changer. She can no longer be a victim; nor will she
ever repeat this scenario. She has taken back her significant
power and is rebuilding her life. I have so much respect for
Elyssa precisely because she has had the courage to dig deep
and find her part in the creation of this reality. This, along
with her clear, strong, very engaging voice, her wonderful
sense of humor, her powerful practicality and her deep gen-
erosity gives her the full credentials to be a way-shower for
women and she is so needed.

It's been two hundred and thirty years since Mary Woll-
stonecraft wrote her seminal work, *A Vindication of the
Rights of Women*. Flash forward to #Me Too and the silence
breakers. The more empowered we become the less possible
are these stories. The more aware, the less likely the wool
can be pulled over our eyes. The more we share our stories,
our lessons and realizations and our pathways to power the
closer we come to a world without oppression.

There is a momentum building towards equality, which will
benefit all people and this book could not be more timely.

Stephanie Sinclaire Lightsmith
Author, *Creative Alchemy: The Science of Miracles*
March, 2020

Introduction

In my past life I spent a lot of time holding my breath–literally and figuratively. This was my way of being "not there." I made myself teeny-tiny, since he was acting really B-I-G (and not in a good way). (He being my ex-husband.)

So how did I come to choose to live small? Well, in the beginning of the relationship, I didn't feel small. Not teeny-tiny small, anyway. Maybe smallish.

In the beginning, he was charming, engaging, good-looking, spontaneous, and romantic. He made me believe I was the center of his world. As I had recently moved to New Zealand for work, I felt smallish, dislocated–and he made me feel bigger.

It wasn't until later that I learned he, not me, was the center of his world, and there actually wasn't room for the two of us. I was just his "food source." I will go into more of details about what I mean by that later, but by now I am sure you are beginning to wonder what I got from him in return for making myself pretty much invisible.

At the time, I believed the main things he provided to me were love, connection and the ability to keep our family together. We had a son together. None of which turned out to be true, but that was the story I told myself, the story around why I couldn't, just couldn't, leave. (Stories are the things we create or adopt as our own–once again, more on this later).

The problem with living teeny-tiny life was, I got so good at being small, I forgot who I was. And when you forget who you are, anything, and I mean *anything*, can happen. And none of it is good.

I write from experience. Effectively, when a person chooses to live with emotional abuse, (often referred to as intimate partner terrorism or emotional terrorism, and defined as a pattern of physical and non-physical violence intended to exert power and control over another person),–putting your life in the hands of an abusive person (call them an abuser, a narcissist, a covert aggressor, a psychopath or a sociopath)– they are choosing to roll the dice.

Think about that: Rolling the dice *on their life*.

Let me tell you, it takes a really, really long time to get to know someone. And when you are with a narcissist, socio-path or psychopath, you can never, ever know them. Not in the way it matters. Not in the way you would ever want.

To make a long story short, in losing myself, I lost every-thing at that time. Literally everything: my son (yes, in the end, I left New Zealand and my son, in order to recover), my family, my financial security, my home and my life as I knew it. I lost a lifetime of dreams, plans and work.

Pause, just a moment…

Does this situation, my former situation, sound heartbreak-ingly familiar?

Are you ready to admit—if now, only to yourself and the pages of this book—that you are in an unhealthy, mind-f#*king, confidence-stealing, terror-inspiring relationship of your own?

Did you too think s/he would hold you up, breathe love and support into you, only to knock you down with words, violence and intimidation?

Are you are feeling an overwhelming fear of what "life after" your own abusive relationship might hold for you, IF you are able to make the choice to leave it?

Hey, there's absolutely no need to deny what may be your everyday reality out of shame or fear. *There's no judgment here. Only compassion.*

I GET IT.

I KNOW where you are, too: Trapped. Lost. Alone. Brain-sick. Body-sick.

And I also can tell you this…*There IS a way out. A journey back to self-love and self-worth! A journey back to a mind-blowingly, energetic, exceedingly powerful version of YOU.*

Short-Track Back to Your Power!!
The purpose of this book and the steps back to you is to short-track your trip back. Back into your power. Back to the AMAZING person you already are.

The power of THE AMAZING YOU.

Like a caterpillar preparing itself for radical transformation, you too will emerge from a shiny, protective casing, radically transform and emerge as the lovely, beautiful, so-much-to-offer-to-the-world, limitless you who you already are. You will be at peace with who you are.

You will be fully at peace with the world around you.

You will be in charge and in control of your destiny, self-aware, happy, vibrant, full of vitality and confidence, and most importantly, full of self-love.

Sounds good, right?

A Personal Invite
I am asking YOU to come with me on a journey. A purposeful journey, to find the thing that was never really lost, the thing that abuse stripped you of: You. It's right there.

It's in your heart just waiting for you to find the tools to set it free.

About My Choice to Share
For years, I struggled about whether or not to write about MY experience—and what I have learned through all of it. I have to tell you, that I am still hesitant about publishing this book, even though it's written. I don't like to "lay it all out there" (although I am getting better at this)! I don't like to be judged...and that's just what I fear may happen.

Another huge factor is my son. My abusive ex-husband is his father, so will the publication of this book affect him, and how? Will he be hurt? Will he hate me for speaking up??

On the flip side, I considered this: I don't want my son, or anyone whom I know, or even don't know for that matter, to choose the path I chose. To spend years of their life the way I have spent these past, way too many years.

So finally, I came to this conclusion: *If I can stop anyone, from choosing this path, from losing themselves; if I can help someone, or many people get back to themselves sooner and gain one, two or ten years of their life back, then I pretty much have an obligation to share my experience.*

In Crushing Fleas I share parts of my unhealthy relationship story… but mostly I share what I have learned after spending literally hundreds of thousands of dollars–and hundreds, if not thousands, of hours–*getting back to peace, getting back to love, self-love and getting back to ME.*

Self-Love and Peace

Once again, I have love–self-love. A sense of overwhelming peace. That was something I had lost by choosing to live a life not guided by my integrity. And this situation, this loss, continued even after he left. (Yes, that may come as a bit of a shocker: HE left ME.)

After he tossed me aside, I saw me as "the victim" for a long, very long time. HIS victim. It took a crazy long time, but eventually I learned that's another **way NOT to live.**

In playing "the victim," we are giving away all of our power, sending it right back to our abuser. We give it to him or her. And, in playing the victim, a person simply cannot get back to who he or she is.

So I write this book in the genuine hope that maybe I can short-track some of the work, pain and expense for you—allowing you to connect the dots faster.
The good news is: *What you can look forward to when you finally get back to YOU…is a happy ending. An even better version of you.*

And you can breathe. You can breathe a lot. Wherever you want. Whenever you want. As freakin' loud as you want.

Breathe and get back you.

PART 1

Living with fleas

Perpetrators of emotional abuse commit emotional rape. They rob the victim of their sense of self as well as the physical things that make them who they are–their home, their financial independence and/or their children–you name it, they take it. Power and control is the name of their game.

Perpetrators of emotional terrorism (as it is also often referred to) should be held accountable. And if you think this is a female problem–men exerting power and control over women–some studies show that men are almost just as likely as women to be abused emotionally during their lifetime. Statistically, thirty percent of women will become victims of emotional terrorism over their lifetime, and twenty percent of men.

In Part 1 of this book, I give you some insight into what happened to me, I describe the significance of fleas, and what emotional terrorism looks like. I also share how to know if you are living with a malignant narcissist, psychopath or sociopath–how to know you are living with fleas.

Emotional abuse is multi-layered and although perpetrators of emotional terrorism can physically abuse their victims, it's the wake of mental and spiritual destruction they leave behind them that is so much more difficult for their victims to recover from.

In Part 2
I share a step-by-step guide back to peace, self-love and The Amazing You–a guide back to a bug-free life!

ONE

Discarded...

Desperate. Ferociously desperate.

This is the feeling I had when my husband said he was leaving me two days before my fortieth birthday. He ranted around the house in full rage, repeating, "I am going to finally do something for MYSELF, Elyssa!"

(When narcissists, psychopaths and sociopaths discard you they will find the most dramatic ways to do it.)

What was my reaction? I got down on my knees and I begged. I begged him not to leave. On my knees, holding our five year old son in my arms, I begged him to stay. Head down in servitude, with tear-filled eyes, promised him that I would be "good." I would do what he said. I would stay in New Zealand (before we were married, we had agreed that we'd return to the USA, my home country). I would be happy with his terms.

As it turned out, part of those terms would end up being that I not leave the country to return to my birth country, the United States, with our son. My ex, whom I will not specifically name in this work, actually had stolen my passport, and taken our son's as well, so that my son and I could not leave the country. He also had shut down my access to our accounts–bank, credit cards, etc. These were the accounts that held 100 percent of our money, of which I had earned 85 percent.

Now, at the time, in addition to our family home, we had five rental properties and a vacation home.

You see, I was one of those security seeking types, and together my ex and I had a plan. I earned a very good living as a digital consultant and the ex had a painting business. Together (at least I thought) we made a very good team. I would be the main breadwinner and he would use his connections to renovate and build rental properties.

Over the years and unbeknown to me, the ex had placed the majority of these properties in a trust under his name, not mine (more on this later, but suffice to write I didn't completely realize this situation at the time). So this man, whom I had once trusted, would be stealing our life's work, and I would be destitute.

As the ex walked out the door, suitcase in hand, I wailed loudly. I was reeling from the pain of my broken soul–the soul he broke.

Who would I be without him? Nothing. Or so I thought back then.

But as flat-out terrifying as it was, that day of desperation marked the beginning of the journey back to me. It marked the beginning of a reawakening, and a radical transformation. It took a lot of hard work, answer-seeking and discarding of old stories, but ultimately I found peace and a greater love of myself than I had ever experienced. That's how it turned out.

How did I get there? That's just what this book is about.

But first....I'm going to have to write about something that makes some of us squirm. Or shriek. Or recoil. Or scratch ourselves uncontrollably.

Or maybe even use the vacuum on!

TWO

About the fleas (and crushing them!)

I am going to do a quick fast forward to 2017 to tell you the significance of fleas (and the title of this book). It's a leap, but stay with me here.

My ex's ability to wield his power got stronger after he left me. Throughout the divorce process, he kept winning: the power, the control, the money, more custody of our son. He took it all, without remorse, without a thought of the impact on me, or our son.

And because he had become so large and powerful, the fear and the anxiety controlled my life. I didn't know what it was at the time, but as a result of the emotional abuse I endured, and continued to endure, I was suffering from Post-Traumatic Stress Disorder.

For years I had sought answers to my symptoms of extreme, overwhelming anxiety and never ending fear. I sought answers that no health worker in New Zealand was able to give me. So in 2013, I made the unthinkable decision to leave my son, the center of my world, and go back to the US to recover. To me, the intensity of my situation was very clear, and I had a choice to make: Leave or die.

Back in the USA, the first psychologist I met with told me she believed I was suffering from Post Traumatic Stress Disorder. When I described what had happened to me, the extent of the abuse, and that I believed I was married to a Narcissist, she said, that although she was unable to diagnose my ex, she thought my ex's behaviors sounded like narcissism bordering on sociopathy.

We will get to a deeper explanation of narcissism later in the book. For now, this validation from a professional, both in terms of what was causing my body to be on fire 24/7, as well as the confirmation that the actions of my ex were well beyond what "normal" looks like in any relationship, gave me the small crumb of hope I needed to begin taking extreme actions towards healing.

Four years later, I had to return to New Zealand for court. As you can imagine, the thought of returning to New Zealand completely terrified me. In my mind, I called New Zealand the "place of rape." Which, actually, it was. The laws in the country (or lack of them) at that time as well as attitudes towards and the miss-understanding of emotional abuse in the mental health care and family court system effectively allowed my ex-husband to rape me of everything I was, both emotionally and physically. (I'll discuss what happened in later chapters so you know how to avoid such a situation in your own life!)

Although I had come a long way, I was still his victim. Four years later I was still giving my power away to him. What else might he do to me? I fretted. I didn't know, but I knew what he was capable of–and I was scared. The anxiety was crucifying.

As I got off the plane at Auckland Airport in New Zealand, familiar tears of grief slid quietly down my cheeks and neck. Although I desperately wanted to see my son (who had been to the USA every summer and winter break up until this time), I was panicking to myself, "What the f#*k am I doing back here? How am I going to make it through the next couple of weeks???"

As I approached the customs agent, he looked at me like I was a criminal. In an aggressive tone he asked me what I was doing in New Zealand.

Through a flood of unstoppable tears–embarrassed–I told him I was coming to see my son. He searched my wet eyes for something more sinister before stamping my passport and nodding me on through.

At that moment my nervous system went into overdrive!! I had to think fast about how I would make it down the hallway without collapsing. And like it was a gift the universe had just handed to me, I had this image of my ex as a flea in my mind. And when I did?

I squashed him!

(True story…)

I literally squashed him underneath the bottom of my shoe right there in the hallway. Hey, I'm sure this looked pretty odd at the time: A woman with a wet face squishing an imaginary bug on the floor. But what I had discovered by then is that visualization in recovery is an important tool. Visualization helps retrain your brain.

And then, being in New Zealand and all (that's where the famous movie "Lord of the Rings" was filmed), I thought of one character in particular, the stunning and amazing half-elven Arwen (played by Liv Tyler), galloping through the fiords with her elfin-like warrior friends on their beautiful horses. And I imagined myself as her, with the stallion I was riding whinnying and rearing, then squashing my ex again and again—squashing that minuscule, bothersome flea.

And that was it: For the rest of the trip, every time I thought of my ex, I thought of him as the flea that he is, and me as the warrior princess that I am.

So for the remainder of this book, I will continue to refer to those who are covert aggressors, psychopaths, sociopaths, narcissists and the like—perpetrators of emotional terrorism—as "fleas." NOT because it's an exercise in name-calling or victim-hood, but because I hope the image that worked for me will now bring a bit of comic relief to what has otherwise been a terrible experience for you.

By no means do I want to belittle your experience, but I do hope the flea analogy used throughout this book will make some of the truths outlined in this book a little more digestible, and possibly humorous.

And eventually, believe it or not, you too will come to think of your ex as just that: an annoying flea. Even if s/he is still trying to suck the lifeblood out of you years after you left (fleas are hard to get rid of), you will be too powerful to let that happen.

You will no longer be their victim, because you will be completely in charge of YOU.

THREE

An answer to how emotional abuse works

Before we get to the steps that take you back to The Amazing You, I know there are a few burning questions you have that need answering. I know, because I asked the same questions for years and years, and no one could answer them for me.

- *How does psychological and emotional abuse work? And more specifically, how did it work it's magic on me? How did my perception of myself change so dramatically?*

- *Why do we stay? Why did I stay?*

After the flea left, these questions ran through my mind all day and all night. For years the ensuing anxiety ensured sleep was a luxury I enjoyed only after I partook in a glass or two of wine and sleeping pills.

In my search for answers, I found many books that described the cycle of emotional abuse–idealization, then devaluation and discard. And after reading and researching these phases, the phases of abuse made real sense to me in terms of the pattern that my relationship went through (we will dive deeper into the Abuse Cycle in the next chapter). But the Cycle of Abuse still didn't answer my deeper question how did someone that seemed so loving, take over my mind and have such a huge impact on my sense of self–my perception of who I was?

A major breakthrough in my discovery process, and part of the answer to my first question about how abuse works to change your perception of yourself so dramatically occurred while I was attending a seminar presented on emotional intelligence.

Emotional intelligence is the ability to be aware of, manage and regulate your emotions as well as be empathetic to the emotions of others.

At one point in the Seminar, we began discussing the fact that if you hear something enough, it becomes a belief. After those words were spoken, I didn't hear much more. **I suddenly, in that moment, had my answer–at least in part–about how emotional abuse works. Words have power. Words have the power to change your brain. They have the power to change how you think about yourself and the world around you.**

"If you tell a lie big enough, loud enough, and long enough, sooner or later people believe it." **–Adolph Hitler**

Word Power
Words have a power that goes way beyond words.

With the right (or wrong!) words, you can become someone unrecognizable, even to yourself.

(If you hear something enough, it becomes a belief.)

Words can change your belief system.

Words can retrain your brain.

And there was my answer. The flea had devalued me by retraining my brain with his words to think I was nothing, and that he was so much more than just a flea.

Squash.

Due to the insight this seminar had offered, I suddenly knew just how it was that my perception of myself had changed from a competent, smart, lovable, independent, fun, attractive person to--Without him, I am nothing.

Dig deep, wherever you are in your relationship, and discover the power of words. Both the bad....AND the good.

Not only can words create a cult of two, between you and your intimate partner, words have in fact fueled the creation of cults (and systems of abuse) that are thousands strong. Words have ignited hate that has divided nations, and words have been the justification for heinous crimes against humanity, such as Hitler with the Holocaust.

On the flip side, words have also empowered some of the most powerful, engaging, lovable figures on earth. Read the words of boxer Muhammad Ali, a true master of words:

"I am the greatest I said that even before I knew I was. I figured that if I said it enough, I would convince the world that I really was the greatest." – **Muhammad Ali**

Muhammad Ali not only physically worked hard to become the greatest fighter on earth, his words had an amazing power.

He had convinced himself, along with the world, that he was the GREATEST FIGHTER ON EARTH with his words. And for a period of time, he actually was! An Olympic gold medalist and a champion boxer, Ali was the first fighter to capture the heavyweight title three times.

Whether it was Ali's intention or not, he had trained his brain as hard as he trained his body.

Self-talk is a very powerful thing, indeed. And so are the words of others.

As another example of the power of words, take the case of Immacule Ilibagiza, author of *Left to Tell: Discovering God Amidst the Rwandan Holocaust,* and whom I heard talk.

Ilibagiza survived the Rwandan Holocaust by hiding in a three-foot-by-four-foot bathroom for ninety-one days while her family and friends, members of the Tutsis, were slaughtered around her.

In her talk, Immacule Ilibagiza spoke about the fact that the Hutus had been planning this Holocaust for generations.

You see, unfortunately, the Hutus understood the power of words. And in preparation for this mass genocide, the Hutu majority government created a national radio station which had, as one of its objectives, to reduce public perception of the Tutsis to cockroach status—through words. Historically, the only real difference between Hutus and Tutsis was economic, not ethnic. The Tutsis, as cattle herders, were generally wealthier then the Hutus. Hutus were farmers and as a generalization less affluent.

Through messages shared by the Hutu led Government, enough of the Hutus adopted the belief that the Tutsis really were nothing but cockroaches–so, *"Why not murder them?"*

Well-educated individuals were involved in this genocide: lawyers, doctors, and people whom you would think would have better judgement. They were regular, smart, educated people.

Tony Robbins and Chloe Madanes, the founders of Strategic Intervention, also talk extensively about the power of words in relationships and notably the power that one human being can wield over another just by introducing thoughts, through their words, into a relationship.

In her book, *Relationship Breakthrough: How to Create Outstanding Relationships In Every Area of You Life,* Madanes talks about the concept of Indirect Influence and the power of Induction. "The attempt to regulate the inner life of another person in order to preserve our own." In order to wield the power of indirect influence we make statements (or as Madanes refers to them "instructions") and assign them to other people. For example, just saying, "You are sad" creates the feeling of sadness in another person.

According to Madanes, "The root of all violence in the world is negative induction: projecting negative values such as "evil" or "dangerous" on other **individuals, groups or**

nations. It is also the root of much suffering."

Words can affect communities and nations. And yes, words have an impact on even smart, self-assured, powerful individuals who are involved in abusive relationships.

Abusers train our brains with their words.

Was I crazy? Was I weak? Was I broken?
No. I wasn't broken. *And neither are you.*
If you hear something enough, it becomes a belief.

That discovery of the power of words set me free!!!
I wasn't like what my ex had played on repeat over the years about me:

- I wasn't "unable to make friends."
- I wasn't "incompetent with money."
- I wasn't "broken."
- I wasn't "undesirable."
- I wasn't "crazy."
- I wasn't "too demanding."
- I wasn't "insecure."
- I wasn't "unsupported by my family."
- I wasn't "incapable of standing on my own two feet."

I trusted my husband–SHOCKER! And because I trusted him, his words had a great power over me.

Through the words my ex used (and the system of abuse he created, which we will get to in the next chapter), I was transformed, overwhelmed with fear, no longer had any idea who I really was, or how I was going to cope with my new painful daily reality.

By the time the flea left, I believed at my core that I really was nothing with, or without him. Through his words, he had taken from me the very essence of who I was–he had taken my soul and the chronic sick feeling in my body, this heightened state of *fear mixed with anxiety, was a result of C-PTSD. (We will get the explanation of what C-PTSD is too!)*

But, through this realization, the realization of the power of words, and the influence people can have over you (your mind, body and soul) through their words, I had hope. I knew then it was possible to retrain my brain back and become razor focused on owning Amazing.

Retraining my brain became my obsession.

Through hard work and DAILY PRACTICE, I would re-find my soul –I would rediscover ME.

FOUR

The flea circus and why we stay

"Just gonna stand there and watch me burn
Well that's alright because I like the way it hurts
Just gonna stand there and hear me cry
Well that's alright because I love the way you lie
I love the way you lie
I love the way you lie"

"I Love the Way You Lie," ~Skylar Grey

Once I had grasped the power of words, and came to understand that fleas use words to mentally change how we think about ourselves, to devalue us, I wanted to know MORE. I still had unanswered questions, in particular: *Why is it so hard to get rid of fleas? I mean, if someone is beating up another person mentally and possibly physically, on a daily basis, why would anyone stay with that flea?*

My desire to find answers to this next question: Why do people stay in this horrible cycle? Why did I stay?–led me to look deeper into abuse and the Abuse Cycle mentioned earlier and here is what I learned.

Abuse Cycle Stage #1: Idealization and Love-Bombing

Your flea needs you. It needs you for narcissistic supply. Narcissistic supply is their "fuel." The term "fuel" was actually coined by the self-proclaimed malignant narcissist himself, H. G. Tudor. According to H. G Tudor, fuel is attention. It can be negative attention or positive attention. For malignant narcissists, negative attention can be even more satisfying. They use this attention to fill the giant hole in their heart. To self-soothe. Without this "narcissistic supply–their fuel" the flea can't survive and so, will do ANYTHING to get it. So the first thing on any flea's agenda is to make sure you fall in love with them so you will supply them with fuel. They need your power. That's right. You are powerful. That's why they chose you.

The flea pulls you in through what is called "love-bombing" and creates a level of attachment that is truly storybook. It's like the ideal relationship out of your favorite romance novel! *It's through this initial whirlwind of supposed love that fleas establish a trusting bond with you so they can drive forward, or induce and maintain, your addiction to them.*

During the love-bombing phase, the flea is everything, simply everything you dreamed of finding in a partner as a little boy or girl, mirroring exactly what you, in your heart of hearts, want to see.

Unfortunately, the love-bombing bond sets you up for all kinds of pain: You spend the first part of your relationship telling people what a "wonderful!" flea you have found and that you are truly in love. However, the love and trust that the flea established with you is based on false pretenses; *it's not real.* So, when the mind games begin, and begin they will, three things occur:

1. You can't explain the change to those around you. (Remember you used to say to everyone how "wonderful!" the flea was?) You now feel shame as a result of the change;

2. You assume that the abuse the flea perpetrates and their malignant behavior is partly your fault. When s/he starts telling you that "you suck" (devaluation), you think it must be true as the flea can be so wonderful at times; and,

3. You are hooked in by the trauma bond that has now been created. The trauma bond is formed as you are

now yearning for that "other them" you knew in the beginning—the good flea, if there is such a thing—to make another appearance. (But that version of the flea is a fake. They only mirrored exactly what you wanted to hear in order to trap you in their web.)

My experience of Idealization and Love-bombing with the ex went something like this.

We didn't hit it off right away: He was just too "over-the-top" when we first met through a mutual friend at a barbecue. He literally strutted like John Travolta in Saturday Night Fever, leather jacket included, plus I had no intention of staying in New Zealand longer than it took for the 2001 technology crash in the US to heal and jobs to become more available again. At the time, I was earning a very good income as a digital consultant in New Zealand.

But the flea was committed to the goal of winning me over. (After all, I was his future cash cow and power supply!) He showed up everywhere I went. He kept busy asking our mutual friends about my whereabouts. Then he showed up at breakfasts, at lunches, and at parties I attended.

When he doggedly continued his pursuit of me, I began to weaken. I noticed he had the most beautiful blue-green eyes, and his obsession with me made me feel, well, wanted and loved. So when he eventually invited me for a coffee, I accepted. He picked me up in a beaten-up and filthy red painting truck; it stunk of old paint and body odor.

We went to a popular café in Wellington. I had already rehearsed my, "I am not staying in New Zealand, so there is no point in dating," speech. But his over-the-top positivity was alluring. As I continued speaking, "… and therefore there is no point in dating me, as I don't want to stay here," my words went through one of the flea's small ears and out the other. When he abruptly got up, paid the bill at the register and walked out the door, I followed him.

We walked up to a memorial in Wellington that looked over the sea on a windy but sunny day. He came up behind me, put his big leather-jacketed arms around me and kissed the side of my head. And that was it: the filthy truck, his amped-up, coffee-overloaded body, his small ears (the true hallmark of a flea?!!)–all warning signs that I ignored.

And so it was: The end of life as I knew it. The end of the "me" that I knew.

Abuse Cycle Stage #2: Devaluation

The next phase of abuse is devaluation. This is where the abusers begin to use **words** and various other manipulation tactics to break you down, isolate you and control you.

Devaluation by a narcissist or sociopath takes many forms. And as stated before, at the center of the abuse is their desire to control you and have power over you so they suck their narcissistic supply from you. They will employ any kind of manipulation tactics to control you. The more they know you, the more they know how to push your buttons and the more information they have to use against you. In summary.

Devaluation can include a number of activities to gain and maintain power and control over you. For example:

Manipulation
Fear
Threats
Physical violence or the threat of physical violence
Intimidation
Mind games
Lies
Martyrdom (poor me)
Calling you crazy/Making you feel crazy
(often referred to as gaslighting)
Isolation tactics
Financial control
Controlling relationships with your children

Establishing An Abusive System Around You

Next, to lock you into their abusive world and devalue even further, the flea uses these tactics to also create an abusive system. The purpose of this system is, again, to take away your power and firm up their grip on you.

Through the flea's lies, the people in your immediate circle become, in a sense, the flea's "puppets." *While s/he's abusing you, the flea is also spreading false information "in confidence" to those people close to you.* In short, the abuse EXTENDS BEYOND the relationship between you and the flea, thus making the abusive situation even harder for you to escape from and/or make sense out of.

His family, your friends, maybe even YOUR FAMILY now are all part of the abusive system the flea has created to keep you trapped – it's a flea circus, but it's neither entertaining nor funny; it's a horrible merry-go-round. It's a system that leaves you feeling even crazier because the whispers you are hearing around you, about you are real and NOT real.

In my case, it was only after the flea left that I realized the extent of the flea's system of lies. And do you know how I figured it out? In New Zealand, if you are seeking a divorce, you are required to go to counseling for a period of time after the two of you separate. So there is usually counseling on your own, as well as couple's counseling. So the flea and I saw the counselor separately. Well, at one point during this period of counseling, the counselor shared with me her amazement over how "different" my story was compared to the flea's version. The flea's story about what had transpired between us apparently had been totally, dramatically different than my version.

This comment knocked my unconscious intuition straight into my consciousness. *What the he#$@ was the ex saying to the counselor? I had no freakin' clue, but it certainly wasn't what actually happened!*

This unexpected insight made me begin to look at previous experiences with the flea, as well as the flea himself through a totally different lens.

Importantly, no one is safe from a narcissist's, psychopath's or sociopath's negative talk, triangulation tactics and lies, all in the name of boosting their fragile ego and knocking yours down.

Abuse Stage #3: Discard

Now that we've covered-off idealization and devaluation, the final stage in the abuse cycle is discard. This is when the flea decides they can no longer get the "narcissistic supply" they require from you (in other words, you aren't giving them what they need, which is fuel–they need to pursue a more plentiful source), and they discard you–whether that means leaving you, cheating on you, giving you the silent treatment or discarding you in some other different but heart-rending way.

Fleas involve you in the abuse cycle on more than one level, too:

- On a macro-level, your relationship will follow this overall pattern of the abuse cycle. The first stage of your relationship is love-bombing or idealization. This is the time when the flea is "Mr. or Ms. Wonderful." The next phase is when s/he will devalue you with words and the system of abuse around you. Then at some point, once you stop feeding his/her need for supply, s/he will discard you. This pattern could go on for months or years before the flea finally discards you for good (or you leave the flea).

- On a micro-level, s/he will engage in the abuse cycle on a daily basis. The flea will tell you things like he loves you and will never leave you, and then make you feel like dirt, stop talking to you, then engage with you like nothing happened, in a matter of hours or even minutes.

The covert aggressor's love-hate game gives them great pleasure, while it leaves you feeling miserable, in a state of high alert, and confused. The end result is you end up feeling crazy. That's why it's called "Crazy-Making"

This Crazy Making is how you lose yourself and your sense of right and wrong, what is made up by the flea for manipulation purposes and what is your truth. You become unable to distinguish what is normal behavior and what is not normal behavior.

Finally, The Answer to Why We Stay

And horribly there in lies the answer to why we stay. The abuse cycle is POWERFUL. Through this abuse cycle, we become addicted to the flea. The addiction looks like this. ***Through such love-then hate-then love patterns (idealization, devaluation and discard), your flea addicts you to them. Just when you think you've had enough, the flea will do something endearing to suck you back into their "story."*** As a result you keep frantically pressing the lever for that one jelly bean that only appears some of the time, just like a rat in a cage will do. The resulting hormone "brouhaha" that is created in your body from high levels of the stress hormone cortisol and then the pleasure hormone dopamine (that comes about when the flea does something to redeem themselves) creates an actual physical addiction.

Yes, as disgusting as it is for me to write this, the intermittent reinforcement of reward and punishment physically, mentally and emotionally addicts you to the flea. This is what is called the "trauma bond," and it's one reason why it is so hard to get rid of fleas.

As an example of just how strong the trauma bond is, look at some Facebook groups for people who are experiencing or have left an abusive relationship. You will see so many examples of amazing women and men–whether they be doctors, lawyers, or artists—putting up with the most outlandishly cruel behavior and making excuses for their flea. Frequently they post comments like, "S/he says s/he loves me, and s/he has such a good side, so it's killing me that I called the police when s/he punched me in the face." In other posts, victims share texts where the flea is begging them to come back using the most desperate of displays of affection and/or cruelly cutting them to pieces. Individuals in the throes of abuse will often ask the group for reassurance as to whether or not the physical abuse and/or emotional abuse is normal behavior.

I can assure you *it is not.*

You will read about people calling emotional abuse "covert abuse." By that they mean, abuse that is harder to "see" and/or catch the abuser in committing the act because it takes the form of subtle putdowns, stalking or pursuing and/or there is no physical mark left.

Yes, narcissists can be quite manipulative and cunning in their pursuit for narcissistic supply. True that!

But abuse is multi-layered. Although some actions of abusers may be covert, others are overt, such as draining joint accounts, and/or or sending through raging text and emails to the abused. In my experience, malignant narcissists employ both covert and overt tactics and it only takes an individual educated in these tactics to spot even the more covertly abusive of fleas.

For example, an abuser can simply park their car next to their target in an otherwise empty parking lot just to reinforce they are "there" to the abused. In their pursuit of narcissistic supply, the covert aggressor knows their mere presence will instill angst in their victim.

And the sad fact is, when you are in the throes of abuse, you defend your flea, even in the most unusual of circumstances. *I know I did.*

By the time it gets that bad, it's what you are used to. You've normalized the behavior in your mind in order to survive it.

It's a defense mechanism. It's also the trauma bond at work.

Here is a helpful diagram of what abuse looks like. After I spent some time mapping this diagram out, truthfully the answer to my question about why we stay is totally obvious!

These fleas strip you of your sense of self and create a POWERFUL SYSTEM OF ABUSE around you. When you add in a dash of addiction and mistaken love, supported by the trauma bond, all based a foundation of trust and locked in by financial control and isolation, you have to then wonder how anyone gets out.

In fact, looking at this diagram should make you realize just how FREAKIN' AMAZING YOU ARE TO HAVE even had the courage to PICK UP THIS BOOK! You ARE AMAZING!

FIVE

So, how do you know you've got fleas?

Clues and red flags

I've just described to you how abuse works, the stages of abuse as well as the power of the trauma bond, and because you have normalized the fleas behavior, you still may be questioning if you have fleas or not. You may still be asking yourself if the way your significant other is treating you is okay or normal.

So how do you know you are with a covert aggressor, narcissist, sociopath or psychopath? How do you know you've got fleas?

Here are examples of abusive behavior that should make you aware that what is going on in your relationship just isn't "normal" and yes, is ABUSIVE. If your intuition starts firing and you are nodding your head "yes" while you read the examples below, you likely have an infestation on your hands.

Love-bombing
- Did the flea tell you that you were "the one" way too fast? Like, the first date, after a few days, a week, a month? Did s/he tell you everything you wanted to hear? Did s/he chase you around like a flea in hot pursuit of a host without even knowing very much about you? Does s/he seem too good to be true?

Isolation and Dependency
- Have you stopped seeing family and friends to meet your partner's needs? When your brother or sister wants to hang out, does the flea tell you that you need to spend time with them, and not your family?

Do they tell you to go out with your friends and then suddenly require you to change your plans? Do they tell you that you aren't good at making friends or don't have any friend? Do they tell you your family isn't close to you or doesn't like you and/or belittle your family.

- Do you feel out of place around their family and friends or your family and friends? Like they are whispering behind your back?

- Does your flea constantly belittle you? Does s/he make fun of your creative inspirations, laugh meanly at your mistakes, and try to point out that s/he is smarter or more educated, or from a better family than you?

- Does your flea call you terms of endearment in front of others, but on the inside you know these are backhanded compliments loaded with negativity?

Financial Control

- Is s/he refusing to let you attend meetings with accountants and lawyers that are managing your accounts? Alternatively do they tell you in the nicest of ways that you don't understand money so they will handle it? Do you have access to your money? Do they refuse to let you work, or sabotage your current job? Do they only "dole out" a certain amount of money to you each week, like you're a child who only gets an allowance? Are they dealing in cash (buying and selling items, doing work for cash) and keeping it for themselves? Do they fly into a rage when you ask about your finances?

Crazy Making

- Are they making nonsensical excuses for their covert actions such as being unavailable for long periods of time, and then blaming you for being too nosy and/or insecure if you probe them for answers?

Lack of Boundaries

- Are they constantly moving boundaries to suit their needs? For example, are they flirtatious with your close friends, but if you so much as look at someone of the opposite sex they fly into a rage. Do they get upset if you're in a meeting or out with a friend and you can't respond to their call right away, but expect an immediate reply from you? Do they call you twenty times a day, or even more?

- Do they blatantly lie, and stick to their lies, even if you prove to them that they just lied!

- Do they make up their own reality such as there are eight days in a week or deny they made commitments that you have clearly documented in writing?

Lack of empathy

- Are they unable to empathize and/or do they invalidate your feelings? For example if you let them know something is hurtful to you, do they fly into a rage, change the subject, twist the story, or tell you that you are too sensitive. Are they unable to accept responsibility for their actions and switching blame back to you or tell you you are crazy for feeling or thinking a certain way? Alternatively do they tell you they would meet that need, only if you could do X, Y and Z that is an impossible criteria to meet? Do they use information about your needs against you and do exactly the complete opposite of what you requested?

Physical Violence or Intimidation
- Does your flea attack you physically such as punching and kicking you? Alternatively do they intimidate you by holding their fist in your face, towering over you or pinning you down? Some fleas are smart and won't want to leave a physical mark on you so they resort these intimidation tactics instead. Other fleas will engage in physical attacks knowing you won't report them or file charges.

These are all typical behaviors of an abuser, covert aggressor, narcissist, psychopath, sociopath–or, as I term it, a flea.

Next, listen to your body. **Unlike the flea, your body DOES NOT lie.** Is there a sick feeling in your heart that is telling you something is very wrong? This is your intuition talking to you. Do you feel overwhelmed with anxiety most of the time? Do you feel fear when you are with your significant other on a regular basis?

These warning signs your body is giving you are also giant red flags. It may seem unusual to you at the moment, but you should not feel sick, fearful and anxious with your significant other! Quite the opposite. You should feel healthy, safe and very well supported.

Now that we've identified some GIANT red flags, it's time to "boil down" what you can expect from allowing your relationship with your flea to continue.

- That amazing person your flea pretends to be at the beginning of your relationship--when they shower you with manufactured attention and promises of unrequited false love doesn't exist. This 'love-bombing' is what they use to lure in their prey.

- Words matter (Chapter 3), and the flea will drip-feed you with words of toxic negativity to break you down, isolate you from your friends and family, and control you financially. Slowly, over time, you will have little idea of the amazing person you once were. You will also begin to feel the effects physically. Your brain and body and soul will become sick.

- They are the smallest of the small. Everything they do is driven by their need to fulfill a giant hole that exists within themselves. They fill this hole with blood–your blood. All they care about is what they need.

- They addict you to them through the abuse cycle (I love you, I hate you, I love you; Chapter 4). You actually become physically addicted to them. The addiction is one of the reasons why it's so hard to leave them.

- Those moments of "nice" that you use to defend them and hold on to as a reason for you to stay are self-serving–serving their need for their narcissistic supply.

- They take pleasure in your pain. When you are breaking down, your flea is feeling "flow"–s/he's getting extreme pleasure from your extreme pain. Normally this would be the kind of flow you feel when you are riding horses, playing golf, or doing the things that you love most.

- Their core desire is to WIN power and control (and in doing so, obtain more narcissistic supply), and ensure that you lose: lose yourself, lose your money, lose your children, lose your integrity, etc. You name it, they want it. They win, and you lose.

- They feel envy, jealously, rage. They do NOT feel empathy, love or any of the positive emotions that you feel. They will do ANYTHING to you to protect their narcissistic supply, and they do so without remorse.

- And very importantly: **You can't fix them.**

- **They will never be the life partner you desire or deserve.**

- **THEY AREN'T WHO YOU THINK THEY ARE.**

This last point is the worst one (hence the "All CAPS"). Or, at least it was for me. The moment that consciously broke my state of denial wide open and I realized the ex was not at all who he pretended to be–that he was a flea, NOT A MAN–occurred a few months after he left. This realization was the moment I truly let go and broke through my bond with the flea. Here is how my moment went.

I met the ex for breakfast during one of the meeting times imposed by the New Zealand family court system. During breakfast, the ex leaned into the table–into my space, and whispered in a sinister voice that I was a f#@king bitch, "The breakup is all your fault."

His diatribe didn't stop there…: "I've been unhappy for years and it's your fault Elyssa. It's your f#@king fault. It's my decision to leave, and I'm not coming back. It's your fault. You are manipulative and difficult. It's your fault. THIS BREAK UP is all your fault you f#@king bitch."

I quietly, breathlessly begged him please to stop, but he continued to rage on, leaning his face closer and closer to mine. His voice directed at me, and me alone, letting me know he was not coming back, and also that if I didn't give him greater visitation rights with our son, he would take me to court for 50/50 custody.

Sanity demanded I create some distance in my mind between him and me that went beyond the length of the table. So for a moment I watched—with heart racing—I watched him from afar, disconnected, trying to make sense of what he was saying—trying to make sense of who this person sitting in front of me was.

He relentlessly continued the abuse, repeating to me I was "manipulative," and that I was "manipulating him right now." (Another tactic used by fleas, they blame the victim.)

"Quit crying!" he demanded.

At that moment, I heard me inside—the me who had to get away. So I stood up to walk out. I looked at the exit door to the cafe: It seemed so far away across the room as families laughed around me, enjoying their morning.

The flea commanded me to sit down immediately—for otherwise I would be showing him I wasn't wanting to work toward reconciliation.

In that buzzing-with-life cafe, I sat down, silent, with pain visibly leaking from my every pore, HEART LODGED IN THROAT. "But you just said you don't want to reconcile," I said quietly back more to me than to him, unheard and confused.

Then, as if everything was normal, the flea looked up, smiled, and waved down the waitress. He said to me in an inappropriately jovial voice, one that was much louder than before so the people seated at the tables around us could hear, "Shall we order breakfast? Come on, eat something. You need to eat."

The evil voice had suddenly disappeared. He was Jekyll and then, in the next moment, he was Hyde.

This was the moment I realized that I had spent the last several years of my life with something terrible—a flea.

During this meeting, the flea made it quite clear he had a few more items to hold over me: custody, money and the promise of reconciliation. He was still in the driver's seat— and what I didn't know then is that he would be for years to come. I wasn't going to be free from him.

When he finally allowed me to leave, I noticed the flea's brother-in-law sitting at another table and watching me as I walked out the door. **The flea had brought part of the flea circus with him to watch the entertainment.**

I drove home crying, shrieking and sobbing in my car, begging God to make it go away—to make him go away. He had me trapped in every way in a prison of his own planning. A prison at the bottom of the earth.

By the time I got home, I was physically ill.

That very night, the flea sent me a text message saying he was sending though some pictures of my son's first day at school, just like nothing had happened earlier that morning. It was another jelly bean. That, and he wanted to make sure I knew he was still there. Watching me, watching my son, watching my actions.

His behaviors, and my body's reactions were quite clear, readers: What was going on was not normal. Not normal at all.

He wasn't who I thought he was.

He was not the person he had pretended to be in the start of our relationship.

He was Hyde—and Jekyll.

You Deserve More Than a Flea

When you come to this point, when you grasp the breadth and depth of their lies and the system of abuse they have created, you will feel physically ill in the stark realization of the evil that fleas are capable of perpetrating. You will realize you can no longer live in denial. You will realize you can no longer sacrifice yourself for a flea.

Your flea, the flea you loved and trusted, is someone entirely different.

This realization is the most devastating element of emotional abuse: The moment when you grasp this reality, the moment when your partner shows their true colors in such a way that you are forced to face the truth about what they really are, you are sent to "rock bottom" to question everything you thought was true and real about the world.

At ground zero, you go on to experience nothing but confusion, grief, despair—and a whole hell of a lot of shame.

To be sure, in the process, it's likely the flea has taken every physical thing from you, like your life-savings, the furnishings and mementos you cherish, indeed your very home, but recovering from the mental devastation is the actually hardest part. And this is the part I think many psychologists, doctors, lawyers, professionals and just the regular run-of-the-mill person miss.

If you are a victim of emotional abuse, sure you are grieving your relationship, like anyone else involved in a divorce or break up. But the effects of abuse are so much more devastating than that. Just when you are thrown into a custody battle or a battle for the money that is rightfully yours, you find yourself…at the bottom, battling for your very soul, the essence of who you are is lost. Your world, your very foundation, makes absolutely no sense. You have no idea who you are or who you once were.

The flea has completed the very thing s/he set out to do.

Mission accomplished. Soul destroyed. Sense of self, gone.

Professionals, family, friends will tell you to be strong, to fight for what is rightfully yours. But on what foundation? In my experience, at this point, without the support you need, you will give anything to the flea, just to keep the peace—the peace you so desperately seek. If you are still stuck in the trauma bond, you will also still be vulnerable to their overtures of possible reconciliation while they have already planned your demise. And worse, you will be thrown into a system that largely doesn't understand the extent to which your abuser will do anything to take you out—all with a charming grin on his/her face.

So What's Next?

I IMPLORE YOU to ask yourself, is this the relationship you deserve? A relationship with a flea?

I think not!

So here in lies the power of this book. The power of the step-by-step guide back to you. Let's get on to Part 2, A Bug-Free Life! This is where I walk you through how I got back ME, and how to approach important house keeping items like how to deal with lawyers, parenting agreements and finances. It is in these steps, that I know, you can embrace the ensuing storm with compassion and love for yourself and own AMAZING!

A PERSONAL ASIDE

How freakin' naive can you be?

As it turns out, very.

So why did I let the flea in? Was I just naive?

I have thought long and very hard about this one. I have spent time with many professional psychologists, coaches, and healers of various modalities investigating the why's. And I have truly searched my soul to understand why. Because I didn't want this to happen again—of course. I didn't want to fall in love with another flea.

More traditional therapists leaned toward Freudian explanations for my predicament. You had a damaged childhood and therefore you were attracted to more of what you already know. You were attracted to the familiar.

And I know this is the experience of some. Some people have experienced abusive, narcissistic parents or brothers, sisters, relatives, influential people in their lives that shaped them…that had a huge impact on who they became as well as the partners they choose. I agree that can happen.

But this explanation just didn't mesh with my childhood experience. It didn't resonate.

My parents were from immigrant families and worked crazy hard for the four of us kids. My Dad was a family first kind of guy. He provided for the family and always included us in big family decisions. He was calm and loving. You had to push him to the absolute limit to get him angry. If you did reach the limit however, you ran!

My mom for the most part was a stay at home Mom. For much of my youth we lived near my Mom's large extended family–five sisters and two brothers and a gaggle of nieces and nephews who were very much a part of our lives. Two of my mom's sisters lived close enough to us that they were often over after school holding their wine symposium on the porch while the cousins ran around and wreaked havoc in our very large back yard and house. I had an amazing grandmother who was always happy and giggling. I called her "Grams." My childhood is filled with great memories of my aunts, uncles, cousins and especially my grandma. There was a lot of love around–especially when you needed it.

My siblings and I were always going to go to College. It wasn't a choice. We were going.

I mean we weren't the Walton's. Of course nothing is perfect. I fought with my three siblings–some more than others. But all in all, I can't say I lacked love or its successors, self confidence and self worth. I certainly can't point to an influential flea that ravaged my sense of self.

So what was it?

I have come to the conclusion that there are two primary reasons for my giant hiccup. First, I was naive. I truly believed my husband would do his best for me and my family, just like my Dad. But the flip side of that was that I lacked discernment. Second, I believed there were certain things in life that you needed to get from a man. I didn't own my own power.

Let's first look at naiveté and discernment.

Of course I had seen the Dateline episode with the psychopath that had cheated people out of millions and/or the sociopath that had beaten their best friend and left them for dead or the woman who's husband physically abused her repeatedly and she still remained with them. But these stories had nothing to do with me. These scenarios all seemed so distant. Sociopaths, Psychopaths, Narcissists–fleas–weren't part of my world. This was the domain of "other people."

I truly believed, based on my experience with my Dad, that my husband was going to do the best for me. Like my father. Family first. I had never been directly exposed to the type of deceit that my flea was capable of perpetrating–the type of deceit that he perpetrated on me.

Next I believed I needed a man to be fulfilled.

I wanted all of those things that we watched in Disney fairy tales. I wanted Prince Charming to sweep me up off my feet and provide for me. I wanted children. I wanted a family and a home. Some things, like money, safety, protection were a man's domain. I needed a man for security. And yes I wanted to love and be loved.

I mean there were warning signs. Right? Warning signs I chose to ignore. Yes.

There was my intuition. At times, screaming "NO" at me. At other times whispering quietly in the vibrations of my soul. Elyssa is this really working for you?

But after I passed some point. And I can't pinpoint when that was– my need to fulfill certain desires, became more important than the whispers–more important than my body pleading with me, "No." I chose to abandon ME.

I cried A LOT during our relationship. I cried too much. Way too much.

I lived in fear. WAY TOO MUCH fear.

But all of this I pushed aside.

Ironically I pushed it aside because of fear. Fear of losing him. Fear of being alone. Fear of not being able to meet someone that wanted to have kids with me before my. Which sounds strange even as I type it. Fear led me to him and "in fear" is how I lived.

Do you get how messed up that is!

So how naive can you be? As it turns out. Very. Yes very.

But the point of this little aside is to share the story.

Share the story so it may normalize your experience.

As Lightsmith pointed out in the Foreword, it's incredibly important to share these stories so that we can collectively become stronger. So that we can collectively say to ourselves,

"You know what? Evil exists." "I am all that I need." And although I can have compassion for the flea in the way that I know he is suffering. I can also say, I don't need to invite you into my life. Because I have DISCERNMENT and I am totally clear about my own power.

Let's teach young women of today exactly that—to be clear about their own power. That they need a man for nothing. If I had discernment and a greater understanding of my own power then, I would have never let him near me.

You have the power. That is why they were attracted to you in the first place.

Own it. Know it.

Trust your judgment.

PART 2

A bug-free life

"On the path of the warrior there is no interruption, the path includes all experiences, both serene and chaotic. Crush them with love. When you experience grief, you will realize love is the only way through to the other side."

Start Where You Are: A Guide to Compassionate Living, Pema Chödrön

Now that we understand how abuse works, why you stayed, and how you know if you have fleas, let's begin with your **after**. Life after fleas.

Fleas, are not in my experience, fixable--and even if they were IT'S CERTAINLY NOT YOUR RESPONSIBILITY TO FIX THEM. It's time to do the work to **FIX YOU– Mind, body and soul.**

It doesn't matter if no one else understands or believes you. The important thing is that I understand and believe you.

It isn't your job to convince anyone else that the person you loved is really just a flea. You know your truth.

The sooner you can reframe your past, and ditch the guilt, shame and victim-hood, the faster you will heal.

So now let's get on—with YOUR future.

As always, I'll be honest and transparent: Achieving your goal of exterminating that flea takes hard work and focus. It takes CHANGING THE WORDS and stories you tell yourself–those stories that s/he repeatedly told you and that are wreaking havoc on your brain and body. It takes practice and repetition to adopt new behavior patterns, new thoughts and positive stories. It also takes removing yourself from the flea, and the negative energy field they have created around you.

It's up to you to do the work. And it's a lifetime engagement. As well as an engagement of a lifetime!

As Chödrön, states "the way through the grief and despair is love." A new found love of THE AMAZING YOU.

And, **if you decide to accept this mission, the mission of reclaiming you and engaging in the steps outlined in this book, you will be well on your way to a BUG-FREE LIFE**.

When you are fully recovered, you will see the flea for what they are: a flea. An annoying buzzy thing that keeps showing up and annoying the hell out of you. But guess what? You will be able to swat the flea like the warrior that you are, with little to no effect on your nervous system.

Sound unbelievable? It's not. My flea is just that: A flea. And I am a beautiful, powerful warrior. So are you.

I did it–and so can you.

Here are the steps you need to take to exterminate the flea—the steps to reawakening and reclaiming you.

The steps to finding peace and self-love. The steps that worked for me.

Step 1:   You are all that you need
Step 2:   Exterminate the flea
Step 3:   Choose a flea-free haven
Step 4:   It's all about the we
Step 5:   Kick anxiety to the curb
Step 6:   Change the story
Step 7:   Practice mindfulness
Step 8:   Nutrition and exercise
Step 9:   Reminder strategies
Step 10: Be wary of lawyers and the legal system
Step 11: Boundaries
Step 12: Highly detailed parenting agreements
Step 13: Get your financial house in order
Step 14: Create your vision
Step 15: Dating
Step 16: Own Amazing !

I will go on to explain the steps to you in the pages that follow. As I do, I will continue to share some of my personal experiences to hopefully help validate your experience.

I also will share some of the advice and learnings from the people I have met along the way. At the end of the steps there are exercises and/or worksheets that will help you to implement what you have read. For some of the exercises,

you will need to visit my website:
http://project336.co

With that, let's begin. Go through these steps in your own
time. Take your time. Take care of you. Be compassionate
with yourself. Remember small steps lead to big change.

Know that there is so much love around you, and the path
you take to get there will be a curving one. Open your
heart, and let's go forth and let's squash some fleas, together.

STEP 1

You are all that you need

Pema Chödrön offers another amazing quote in her book, *Start Where You Are: A Guide to Compassionate Living*:

> "We already have everything we need. There is no reason for self-improvement. All of these trips that we lay on ourselves--the heavy-duty fearing that we're bad and hoping that we're good, the identities that we so dearly cling to, the rage, the jealousy and addictions of all kinds–never touch our basic wealth. They are like clouds that temporarily block the sun. But all the time our warmth and brilliance are right here. This is who we really are."

So where do YOU start? How do you begin again, after all you've been through and endured?

As Chödrön says, start exactly where you are. ***Start from a place of compassion for yourself as a human on this earth. Your awakening is simply an awakening of all that you already are: a warrior.***

Start exactly where you are, without judgment. You are amazing, completely whole, and all that you need.

So who ARE you? Close your eyes. Look beyond anything external. Look beyond your clothes, your skin and the shape of your body to feel your soul. You are right there. All the other junk around you is just that: junk and stories– self-limiting beliefs–created by a flea.

The first step in healing is being aware of the wonderfully perfect version of you. Your soul.

Exercise: *You are all that you need*

Sit with yourself for five minutes. Sit comfortably in a chair, with your eyes closed and your feet grounded on the floor. Really feel your feel on the floor–press them into the floor. Feel the support of the earth underneath them. Take three, long, slow breaths. If it helps, you can count as you breath in for four counts and then as you breath out for six counts and repeat. Continue breathing and then, let yourself feel who you really are. Without judgment.

Can you tap into your soul? Yes, you can: It's right there. That wonderfully perfect you.

Grab that soul with your hand and pull it close to your heart. Pull love into your heart. Into your soul. Keep breathing for as long as you like. Then exhale, with sound. A loud lovely sound. And feel your body relax into love. The love of you.

Protect it. Keep your soul safe because it is all that you need. It is who you are.

STEP 2

Exterminate the flea

"Exterminate??" Yes!!! In other words, get rid of that flea. Your safety, emotional and physical, are of the utmost importance at this time, as is meeting your basic needs for food, water and shelter for you and any children you may have.

Absolutely I don't want to minimize how difficult it is to leave. The act of leaving is HARD. And we've already covered off why it is so damn hard.

Some fleas will make it even harder for you by feeding your addiction and/or begging you to come back. They might be making promises to "fix" themselves and/or telling you how much they "love" you.

Others, if they have found a replacement–a new partner–to secure their narcissistic supply from, will discard you in the cruelest of ways, and then come back into your life after your replacement sees them as the flea that they really are. As you know by now, that's what happened to me: I didn't leave, but I was left (discarded). I can't honestly tell you what the "breaking point" would have been for me, if it ever came at all, that would have made me leave. That's the honest and scary truth.

So believe me, I know it is an unbelievably hard decision when your whole world is vibrating at such a low frequency (we will talk about energy later and the Law of Attraction). The self-doubt and the million-plus-one stories your family or friends or society as a whole may have created to keep you partnered-up is overwhelming. You may also have financial concerns, fear of being alone and/or breaking up your family. And it is scary–terrifying, in fact.

But you need to be committed to your truth. Resolute in knowing s/he is just a flea and you deserve better.

Why? **Because life is beautiful on the other side.**

Financial concerns and the possibility of physical violence is real, so you need to act accordingly.

If you have concerns about violence and finances, call the National Domestic Violence Hotline. They can help you make a plan to keep you and your loved ones safe and point you in the right direction in terms of finding support.

The other stories of the Bridget Jones variety I just mentioned such as the fact you need to be married, or have a significant other, or that you will be alone for the rest of your life living with seven cats, spending Saturday nights in front of the television—that you are not worthy of love, etc., are all just stories–not truth, STORIES–that you are telling yourself. And, thrillingly and wonderfully, there are many, many more partners that are WAY more appealing and lovable…than a flea.

If You Have Kids
What about if you happen to have children? I struggle all the time knowing that my son will always have the flea in his life. But I can tell you from experience children are so

adaptable. They need love first and foremost, and I know that I am being the best mom I can be for my son. And, I am showing him a different way of being–a different, peaceful way of living. A way that involves love and caring and family. A way that involves appropriate boundaries and associated value system.

Be the parent that your children need. Tell them you love them, stay present and have a place for them in your heart bigger than big.

Communicate with children clearly about boundaries and expectations and if you have the resources to do so, seek the support of a child psychologist trained in managing fleas to help you navigate difficult conversations with your child(ren). Remember, if you had a child with an alcoholic parent or someone with another type of personal struggle, you would have the same job on your hands–to raise you children acknowledging that they love their mom or dad, but to be aware of the behaviors that come with a mental illness.

They will thrive in the loving environment you will provide for them. And remember that showing your children what a healthy relationship looks like is crucial to their development.

It is not an easy road, but I am positive that my child is much better off with a happy, mentally thriving mother as a role model.

I know that if I was still with the flea, I would be dead. If not in body, then definitely in mind and soul. Besides being a better, stronger person today, I am a better mother as well for having rid myself of the flea.

There is no greater hell than living a life dictated by a tyrannical flea surrounded by a flea circus. Once you set yourself free from its blood-sucking bite, LIFE will truly begin!!

Exercise: *Exterminate the flea*

If you feel you are at risk in any way, call the National Domestic
Violence Hotline. 1-800-799-7233.

STEP 3

Choose a flea-free haven

Once you decide you have had "enough!" of the flea and are ready to commit to YOU, you will need to exit the toxic world that the flea has built around you and create a new one. When you are ready to leave, you need to find a safe haven away from the flea circus.

Your safe haven is a place where…:

- *You know you are welcome*
- *You can stay until you are ready to move on to the next step*
  (preferably; if you can only find a place for a short-term stay, then that still is preferable to staying with a flea)
- *You feel at peace and that can provide you refuge from the driving fear*
- *It is out of the flea's reach.*

Once I left New Zealand, the only place that I could see myself feeling safe and finding peace was at my brother's and sister-in-law's house. I know this choice was terribly inconvenient for them, but the thought of being anywhere else threw me back into a wild panic. And I thank them for their refuge!

Find the place that suits you and go with it.

Importantly, remind yourself this is a time of gathering and healing for you. Again, treat yourself with love and compassion. Nothing is permanent. You future holds something amazing for you. I am positive about that. Although you may feel very alone at the moment, possibly sad, grieving and/or fearful, sit with yourself and move through the fear. Remember you are totally capable. Remember s/he came to you because you are powerful. Beyond capable, you are AMAZING!

Exercise: *Choose a flea-free haven*

Sit down and think about the place where you feel most comfortable. Do you have the support of family and friends? If not your own home, consider where and with whom would you be able to comfortably stay with while you recover?

If you are able to stay in your own home, make sure you are safe. Alert the local police of your situation if your safety may be at risk and as above, call the National Domestic Violence Hotline at 1-800-799-7233.

If you need to seek the support of a shelter, research what is available in your area.

If you need financial resources, don't be afraid to research and apply for help. Even for things like summer camp or sports for your kids, reach out to local organizations in your area and find out what is available. If you don't ask, you don't get, and there are often many untapped grants and scholarships available to those in temporary need.

STEP 4

It's all about the we

Let me credit sports nutritionist and trainer Vicki Kenney as the one who said, "It's all about the we."

She's right: *You're not alone!! There is strength in numbers.*

It's the two of us. And…It's…:

- You with your friends and family.

- You with a community of support.

- You with professionals who have your back.

It is ever so important to have others helping you on your journey. You have a lot on your plate now that you have left your flea. But rather than dwelling on the flea ever again, dwell on how others can help you stay rid of your flea!!

Doing so is essential to the success of your new choice.

Create a professional support system
It's important to build a trusted network of mentors and professionals. Take your sweet time finding the right professionals to help you. Start scheduling as many (free) "meets-and-greets" as it takes until you find the right psychologist, lawyer, mentor and/or life coach with whom you "gel" and who are **fully schooled in the tactics and the extremes covert aggressors, psychopaths, narcissists, and sociopaths will employ to make sure your life is a living hell and they win**. Note that many professionals will take an initial meeting with you for free.

Word of warning

Because of misinformed or uneducated professionals, thousands of people just like you can end up suffering needlessly. From a legal perspective, you can lose your money, your children and/or find yourself caught in legal agreements or court situations that enable the abuser to continue their abusive behaviors. For example, in my case (handled in the New Zealand courts), I was forced weekly to be in the presence of my abuser even after he left–which meant he could continue to abuse me.

In custody cases like mine, you can end up losing the battle before it even starts. As untrained psychologists or social workers are just as vulnerable to the flea's manipulation tactics and lies.

(We will delve deeper into the importance of working with professionals trained in dealing with abuse and the effects of this trauma in Steps 10, 12 and 13.)

Lean on family and friends

If you have family and/or a network of friends, NOW is the time to reach out to them. (Preferably, they are not connected to the flea.)

A bit of advice: Don't expect them to fully understand what you are going through. Just know that they love you and are doing the best they can.

In New Zealand I had a best friend, so, each day after work I would pick up my son up from school, then inevitably meet with her at her house or mine for a quick cup of tea. Her friendship was a lifesaver.

Find your lifesaver and make their living room yours for a while. Your true friends will be there for you, both during the relationship and after.

Build your community
As humans, we all need connection and love. Finding the right community will help you break old patterns, silence unfounded beliefs in old "stories" and get you away from the flea's system of abuse.

Kenney, the sports nutritionist and trainer I mentioned earlier, shared her experience with me on the importance of community in breaking old habits and addictions. As the manager of a CrossFit gym in Florida, she told me some of her clients were recovering addicts of various types. According to Kenney, the CrossFit workouts enabled these clients to regain their self-confidence while they completed "super-human" tasks like flipping tires or tossing wall balls.

But she told me what was even more critical to their recovery was participating in the gym community. Exercise became their drug of choice, and at the gym they found camaraderie and friendship—a whole new circle of friends that shared their same interests. This is the type of community I desire you to find for yourself.

If the gym isn't your thing, community can be found anywhere—at a coffee shop, for example—and/or by participating in interest groups, recreational sports teams and meet-ups. *I suggest starting with the things that you love doing, and opening yourself up to new experiences. Here are some ideas to get you thinking!*

Baseball
Dungeons and Dragons
Pilates
Technology
Horseback Riding
Golfing
Reading
Potting
Trainspotting
Cars
Writing
Painting
Science
Jewelry Making
Religious Groups
Or maybe you love what you do for a living!

Whatever! It really doesn't matter. The point is to find people of like interests that you can connect with on a REGULAR basis. The more the better. The best scenario–find things you can do almost daily.

Community can be found online too, although only use this medium in a balanced way: Getting out of the house is important to test the waters, to strengthen new brain muscles, to practice elevating yourself, to get about meeting people, and to push through fear and anxiety. Stepping outside of your comfort zone is part of the process of rediscovering The Amazing You.

Afraid of reaching out?
We will discuss this more in the next section, but I can assure you that *everyone out there is looking for connection.* Even though hiding out in your room might seem like your safest and most satisfying choice right now, resist the urge. RESIST!

Isolation is your enemy. Do the opposite: **Reach out.** The chances that someone will say no to a cup of coffee with a person as amazing as you are slim to none.

It's awkward, SOMETIMES. Trying new things and meeting new people is awkward for everyone at times. Keep trying and don't get discouraged. It's a practice. Keep seeking until you find the community that feels like home.

Exercise: *It's all about the we*

Meet with at least three lawyers and three psychologists to begin to understand your options.

1. Contact At Least 3 Lawyers
Many lawyers offer a free initial consultation. Take advantage of this. Find out what may or may not be possible given your particular circumstance and the State or Country you live in. Make sure they understand what a narcissist is and what they are capable of. If you feel uncomfortable at anytime, thank them for their time and LEAVE.

2. Contact At Least 3 Psychologists
Reach out to at least 3 Psychologists that specialize in trauma and understand narcissism and the effects of narcissistic abuse. They may offer a free consultation service as well. They may refer you to their peers once they understand your situation too. That's OK. Again, listen and be open to the possibilities. Once again, if you feel uncomfortable at any time, thank them and leave.

3. Schedule at least 3 outings a week
Knock on the door at the local gym, pilates studio, business meet-up or meditation group. Schedule at least three outings a week and don't quit until you find your community!

STEP 5

Kick anxiety to the curb

If you have been abused, it's possible that you now are suffering from Post-Traumatic Stress Disorder (PTSD) or Complex Post-Traumatic Stress Disorder (C-PTSD). The former is usually associated with one-off traumatic events; the latter is usually associated with trauma that is experienced repeatedly over weeks or years.

PTSD or C-PTSD is what people experience after war, or rape, or experiencing some other form of extreme trauma.

PTSD or C-PTSD is characterized by severe anxiety, nightmares, flashbacks, uncontrollable thoughts of the event(s), rehashing of the event and other super fun symptoms like avoidance of anything that reminds you of the event, where the event took place, trouble sleep and concentrating.

Symptoms can occur immediately or not for years after the event(s) take place, and can be triggered by any event, place, person, thing or activity.

When you are living with fleas, anxiety becomes a way of life. Their behavior is so unpredictable, and this, combined with their crazy-making tactics keeps your sensory nerves on permanent overload. Even when you do your best to "behave," you will find there is no reprieve from the flea's blood-sucking ways for your good behavior.

In many instances, the effects of C-PSTD or PTSD can get worse after you leave. You may also be feeling lost: lost in grief for the loss of your family, lost in the thought of who you are or who you once were, lost in the wondering of how this all happened. **Importantly, insomnia, depression, mood swings, wanting to isolate yourself from family and friends are also symptoms that result from being abused like this.**

You Protecting You

The state of "high-alert" characteristic of PTSD OR C-PTSD is actually you protecting yourself. The response is natural: There aren't any more tigers chasing us around, at least where I live (!), but all humans still have the fight-or-flight response that automatically kicks in when responding to danger. *So when you live with a covert aggressor, narcissist, psychopath or sociopath, your body and mind are on high alert 24/7.*

For me, the anxiety as a result of my C-PTSD was simply unrelenting. Life itself was one endless trigger. I rationalized my way through the days, telling myself it was just anxiety, and wondering if this was just "who I was." *Was I always this way? Was I just an anxious person? Was I just going to live in this state of fear, panic and distress for the rest of my life?"*

I went to several psychologists in New Zealand to try to find answers. I was told all sorts of things, like I "had been anxious all my life" and that my problem was "…just exacerbated by normal divorce tensions with the ex." I was also told I had "simple separation anxiety" from living away from my son part-time. *No one mentioned trauma or C-PTSD/PTSD.* When I became visibly upset in front of the psychologist from the New Zealand Family Court (and she's a real doozy; I discuss her in Step 12), she dismissed me from her office to give me some "time alone" and asked me to return when I was "ready to talk." Apparently my emotional state was disturbing her, and she needed to make a phone call.

My response to her was, "Are you serious?" She confirmed, yes, she was! And kicked me out of her office and began making calls.

TRUE STORY!

Other psychologists I saw offered standard approaches to relieving the anxiety–drugs, worst-case-scenario thinking, taking time out for myself, more talk therapy, etc. All of these recommendations offered only short-term, momentary, Band-aids. I needed a long-term solution, not a massage or pedicure!!! Looking back on it, they really had no idea what I was talking about. From my experience, emotional abuse just wasn't acknowledged by these professionals and neither was PTSD as a result of emotional abuse. What I was experiencing just wasn't recognized as "a thing." And, to make things worse, I didn't have enough confidence to keep searching for the *right help*.

A few years later, after living with C-PTSD on a daily basis, mostly extreme anxiety, and a totally sleep deprived, I ended up on the side of the road in my car in New Zealand, crying and at a total loss for what to do next. I was absolutely desperate for an answer, for some relief!!! I couldn't take another day of the stress: My body was beyond exhausted. My skin, my hair, my eyes, my entire body and internal systems were fragile, overworked and hyper-sensitive. And I had lived this way for years. I finally had to make the choice to leave my son behind and come home to the US to work on my recovery.

I began seeing a therapist upon my return—and almost immediately she told me I had PTSD. Finally my experience was validated! I wasn't deluded or crazy. I wasn't damaged or over-dramatic. I wasn't destined to live in this demoralizing, life-altering, soul-crushing state. I had a real "thing" with a real name.

It was a C-PTSD thing.

And now that I had a diagnosis, I could begin a meaningful discovery process for recovery.

I began therapy specifically for trauma and C-PTSD. The validation of my experience, the talk therapy and exercises for trauma helped and alleviated some of my experience. However, I missed my son terribly and months later, I was still living with daily anxiety mixed with intermittent panic attacks that I had to talk my way out of. It was a struggle, to say the least.

My therapist recommended I try another approach called Neurofeedback. She explained that through this process of I could effectively retrain my brain. Neurofeedback is not for the faint hearted, but definitely for those that like playing video games and watching movies! And I'm not kidding here. (Note this is not a technical description of what it is, but rather my experience of it.) During a Neurofeedback session electrodes are applied to your head so that a technician can monitor your reactions (well your brain's reactions) to a video game or movie. As you sit and play video games using your brain to move images on the screen, instead of a controller, information is fed back to your brain to retrain its response to various stimuli.

OK this is my layman description, but it's somewhat accurate. You watch video games and movies, and your brain gets retrained.

Yes. It's that easy.

The idea of Neurofeedback and retraining my brain to react differently to various triggers made a whole heck of a lot of sense to me after my previous findings about the power of words and how abuse worked to train our brains.

Here was what I thought, in a nutshell:

1. If the ex could train my brain to think I was a "worthless piece of shit," I could certainly train it back to believing that I was "ridiculously amazing, a total badass."

2. In layman's terms, my nervous system was on permanent high-alert, so it made sense to me that I could train a different response. I understood that

living in a state of high alert for so many years had trained my brain to be on high alert even after the threat (the ex) was gone.

3. The brain is a muscle, for gosh sake! *If I can train my body, I can train my brain.*

And at that point in my journey, I was willing to try anything. I wanted to ditch the pain and endless anxiety and own Amazing.

Several Neurofeedback sessions later and I did actually do something amazing. I drove home in the snow without even a thought or a worry or an ounce of anxiety. You might think this is ridiculous; after all, I am a grown woman who crushes fleas, so why would I have an issue with driving in the snow? But yes, in the past, driving in the snow was a huge trigger for my anxiety.

My recent accomplishment dawned on me as I stepped out of the car. I stood up and I jumped for pure joy in my driveway with my arms raised in triumph, like I had just won a gold medal for doing something extraordinary. The change was subtle, but for me, it's impact on how I thought about my anxiety was *PROFOUND*.

In that moment I knew that—with work—I could definitively release myself from the constant fear that wreaked havoc on my daily existence.

Driving home carefree in the snow showed me that overcoming anxiety and the effects of abuse was absolutely within my power. I had a discovered that I actually did have superpowers. It showed me that I was completely in control of me.

So what was the next step for me? I started with changing the stories (as discussed in the next step). *As my stories changed, my energy changed and I began to own my life again.*

I was on the right path to rediscovering The Amazing Me.

Exercise: *Kick anxiety to the curb*

If you think you are suffering from PTSD or C-PTSD or other life-altering symptoms, please seek professional help.

Keep searching for professionals and approaches that work for you. For me, neurofeedback was the push my brain needed to send me on my way to recovery, you may respond more favorably to another method.

STEP 6

Change the story

Now that you have surrounded yourself with love and a supportive system and you've begun to experience some of the benefits of retraining your brain and have alleviated some of your symptoms, the next step is reconnecting with who you really are, your soul. As research professor Dr. Brene Brown tells us in her book, *Braving the Wilderness*:

> True belonging is the spiritual practice of believing in and belonging to yourself so deeply that you can share your most authentic self with the world and find sacredness in both being a part of something and standing alone in the wilderness. ***True belonging doesn't require you to change who you are; it requires you to be who you are.***

If true belonging is achieved by being exactly who you are, how do you reconnect with the warrior right there inside of you??

One giant step in the quest for reclaiming and reconnecting with the AMAZING YOU is dropping the negative stories–the self-limiting beliefs. What I mean by *stories is the things we create or adopt as our own.* Then, there are *facts*. Facts are the things that are known and true.

For example, at this very moment, you may be telling yourself, *I am crazy.* The "I" part is a fact. After all, you are a person. So it's a fact. The "am crazy" part of that statement is part of the story (and a negative story–negative self-talk). It's either your story–*or the story that your abusive flea repeated over and again until you believed it.*

There are also healthy or positive stories. For example, like Muhammad Ali you could tell yourself, I am amazing. And you are. This too is a story, but a positive one you can own for yourself.

We all create or adopt stories, both positive and negative. All of them impact us on a physiological level: They change our brain. They change our energy. What is our energy? I like Jack Canfield's, the Author of *Chicken Soup for the Soul*® series of books, definition the best. Canfield defines the Law of Attraction as:

"The **law of attraction** states that you will attract into your life–whether wanted or unwanted–whatever you give your **energy,** focus, and attention to. You are constantly giving off vibrations of **energy** when you think and feel. These vibrations can be picked up and received by other people."

So when you are telling yourself negative thoughts, you in turn attract negative energy into your life. And perhaps even negative people. It's a self fulfilling prophecy.

In an abusive relationship we are bombarded with stories. Negative stories. This is why we feel sick all of the time. These stories keep our nervous system on high alert and literally change our brains, body and soul. They change our physiology, and lower the frequency of the energy we emit. If we buy into the Law of Attraction as defined by Canfield, if we hang on to negative stories, we in turn attract more negativity because we are vibrating a such a low frequency!

In order to heal, retrain our brain and create radical transformation for ourselves and raise our energy frequency, we need to drop the negative self-talk, the negative stories and replace them with positive ones.

Sound simple? Yes, the concept is indeed simple, but to implement this strategy actually takes a lot, A LOT of practice, repetition, and forcing yourself to do things you haven't done for years. It's a real bitch of a job in the beginning!! But the important thing is to start changing the stories.

Let's look at some typical stories that we hear in an abusive environment—and then, let's leave them to the fleas.

Story #1: "You Do Not Deserve a Place at the Table"
When you leave and start to experience life on your own, you might feel like an alien. I know I did: I felt like an alien in my own skin. I also felt like an outsider in social settings. I told myself I didn't deserve to be there.

BACKTRACK. How did this story all start? Well, for me, the ex always told me that I "…had a hard time making friends." He would reinforce this by leveraging the system of abuse he created around me by telling our friends that I "…had a hard time making friends" in front of me. Then he would also ask his family to take me out socially—because I "…had no friends." So his sister would ask me out socially to hang out with her friends.

The whole thing was degrading and embarrassing. "She has no friends. Can you take her out?"

Over time, I believed him to the point that even at work, I began to feel like an alien. I would sit there and think, Is everyone just better at their jobs other than I am? Does everyone also just relate to one another better? Am I the outsider?

I was actually very good at my job. A key data point was that I was earning bucket loads at the time as an independent consultant. But, even still, the flea had convinced me, slowly, over time, with his drip-feed of painful comments that I was unworthy of my place at the work table. And eventually I just felt like I didn't fit in anywhere.

OVERCOME. How did I overcome this feeling of alienation?

AND THIS PART IS IMPORTANT!

I told myself a different story, then I forced myself to live in that skin.

In my specific case, I reached out to people, and invited them to play golf. Then I went to play golf with them when they accepted. While I was playing golf as an alien outsider, I repeated to myself, I deserve to be here. I belong. I deserve to be here. Through the words and the event, I was practicing NOT feeling like an alien and telling myself I DESERVED A PLACE AT THE TABLE. I was retraining my brain.

Then eventually, after a few golf outings, I built up enough confidence to open my mouth and engage in the conversation. At first I felt awkward, but to my surprise, people engaged in conversations with me right back. (Duh. :-))

And the energy changed. **My energy.** Rather quickly I realized, not only do I deserve a place anywhere that I choose to be, I am pretty likable. Way more likable than the flea, anyhow.

To my readers: This is how deliberate I want you to be while working hard to change your negative stories.

Story #2: "You Are Crazy"

You are NOT crazy. NOT crazy. Not even a little bit. Accept you are not crazy and ignore the naysayers.

F#@K CRAZY!

And believe me, you will come across many naysayers in your search for answers about your experience with abuse. And they will tell you, "You are crazy," either outright or in more subversive or subtle ways.

Accepting that you are NOT crazy and that you have been abused is an important step. DO NOT MINIMIZE WHAT YOU HAVE ENDURED. And don't let anyone tell you differently.

BACKTRACK. No doubt you have heard repeatedly from your abuser just how big of a lunatic you are–along with words like, "bitch, cunt, undeserving, insecure, nosy, worthless, lazy, ugly, fat, friendless, family-less, unable-to-support-yourself piece of shit, no good, loser." We could go on and on.

As discussed above, this verbal throw-up is just the tip of the iceberg. What you are trying to exit is a mental torture chamber (remember it's called EMOTIONAL TERRORISM). And the kicker, is you are trying to exit when your soul has been totally depleted. You are exhausted.

OVERCOME. Accept that the flea, is that—a flea—and it has nothing to do with you.
This is a HEALTHY story. You are not crazy. What s/he did to you has nothing to do with you. You are a warrior. You are Amazing.

Story #3: "You Are Incapable"
Psychopaths, narcissists, covert aggressors and sociopaths trap us through breaking us down and isolating us. When you leave you will most likely feel totally incapable of functioning in the real world because the flea told you, once again with his/her drip-feed of horrible comments, over and again you couldn't, well, function without them.

BACKTRACK. Chances are your flea may have told you something like, "you don't understand money, you aren't very good at much of anything, you couldn't hold a job if your life depended on it," so attending an interview has become the scariest thing on the planet earth.

OVERCOME. Say out loud, "I am amazing at X, or Y" and rinse and repeat those words (maybe even in front of the mirror) in a Wonder Woman power stance (yes this is another "thing"–Wonder Woman power stance), over and again. Warning! At first this exercise may make you cry about how much it hurts that you even believed this about yourself, and then laugh out loud at the same time at the sheer, seemingly ridiculous nature of saying these things out loud. I know I did. But it works.

Trust me.

Next, let's return to the job-related scenario for even more specific advice and guidance as an example of what to do next. As just mentioned, it's important to replace the negative story with the fact that you are totally capable of interviewing for a job. (I'd even go as far to write you will be insanely amazing at it.) But you also need to start practicing how to interview and put your best foot forward. Yes, practicing. You need to be deliberate and committed to your goal in order to change the stories.

And here are some other helpful points that can assist you in changing your story for good:

- **Point #1: Stop ruminating on the past.**
  Psychopaths, narcissists and disordered personality types are just that: disordered! In layman's terms, THEY actually are the "crazy" ones. So trying to make any sense out of what happened is nonsensical. It doesn't work, believe me. I spent far too many

years reviewing, rewinding, replaying, rethinking and ruminating over what happened: How did this happen? Why couldn't I fix it?

The simple fact is, it is THEIR behavior that doesn't make any sense. So stop trying to make order out of chaos. I've tried it. It doesn't work. And it's a waste of your brain power.

The past is the past. Embrace the amazing future you started creating the day you walked out that door.

- **Point #2: Forgive yourself and let go of shame**
  Forgiveness and letting go of the shame is EVERY THING.
  Really!! As the stories in this book demonstrate, everyone on this planet is vulnerable to covert aggressors, psychopaths, sociopaths and narcissists because, by default, humans want to believe people are good at heart. We want to trust. We want to love and be loved. Unfortunately, this pig of a flea decided to prey on you.

You are not broken; you have nothing of which to be ashamed. They do.

Forgive yourself, and accept that you are human.

- **Point #3: Let go of victim-hood.**
  For a very long time I accepted the role as the flea's victim. Too long. Ultimately what I realized was remaining in the role of victim meant that I spent

too many hours giving my power to the flea filling my brain with the whys and the hows and the if only I had...

Once I let go of this role as "broken," I was set FREE. This acceptance of me, myself and I as The Amazing person that I am, freed up my mind to focus on my Amazing future.

I forgave myself and dropped the past so I could live for me...so that I could spend my precious time and sacred brain space developing new positive neural pathways and rediscovering who I was.

Letting go set me free to fill my brain with positive visions of the amazing rest of my life–the life I choose. And I choose Amazing!!

That doesn't mean what the flea did to me didn't happen; it happened. What it does mean is that I don't live in his pain anymore. He can't escape, but I can. And I did: I chose life after the flea. So should you.

And now its time to own your power, your love, your vulnerability. Retraining your brain is a lifetime journey, but once you experience the benefits, you get "hooked "and you just keep seeking out new ways to evolve. How's that for a new POSITIVE addiction?

Soon you will realize that the flea was just telling you stories. And you are in control of creating your own and letting theirs go.

Exercise: *Change the story*

What you think and fill your mind with MATTERS. Your thoughts effect your brain and your body.

Check in with yourself frequently and make note of the stories you are playing in your mind as well as things like the music you listen to and the people you surround yourself with. What are they telling you? How do they make you feel?

Then replace the negative with the positive. Soon you will be emanating at a higher frequency and as a result, attracting higher frequency people and experiences into your life!

STEP 7

Practice mindfulness

Mindfulness practices are another tool in your toolkit for getting rid of all the horrible stories s/he put in your head about who you are. They also greatly assist in relieving anxiety and retraining the brain. Mindfulness practices are fuel that propel you to the next stage of your re-awakening.

So, just what is mindfulness? According to Holistic Healer, Simone Lybarger, mindfulness is awareness. It's knowing what we are thinking and feeling at any given moment. Once we are aware of our thoughts and emotions, we can then choose what thoughts we accept and reject those which don't serve us. That's right: We choose.

We can practice mindfulness at any moment that we feel the need. For example, Lybarger teaches that we can practice being mindful when walking. We can be mindful of how our foot feels as it steps onto the sidewalk; we can be mindful of the smell of the air and the warmth of the sun in the sky. Being mindful connects us with the present.

Mindfulness practices such as meditation, yoga, and breathing will be your salvation and are invaluable tools for retraining your brain. If you accept the mission of calming your brain and recharging and rewiring it with new thoughts, you are accepting a mission of radical transformation. This is what mindfulness practices enable you to do: They enable you to shift your energy and access the true you.

In this chapter we will discuss four practices: meditation, yoga, breathing and visualization. You can choose one or adopt them all as your own. It's really about connecting to what works for your mind, your body and your soul. There is also overlap between these practices. So, for example, in meditation you focus on your breathing, and visualizations are used in focused meditations. As another example, in yoga you use your breath as you move through the poses. There is also mini-meditations at the end of a yoga practice called Shavasana.

Meditation

I learned through my own discovery and practice that there is a reason why all of those Buddhist Monks have a per-ma-grin on their face and speak about love and peace in the world. It's because they have gigantic prefrontal cortexes as a result of meditating!

The prefrontal cortex manages concentration, awareness and decision-making. It's the part of the brain that truly makes homo sapiens one giant evolutionary step beyond the ape. (And light years ahead of fleas.) Think of meditation as an exercise for the most complex organ in your body: your brain.

There are lots of studies available about the benefits, but the long and the short of it is, meditation retrains your brain.

Another great thing about meditation is it's free, and you can do it in your own time. I think of it as a "mini-vacation" for my mind. It provides a vacation from the over-stimulation to which we all have become so used to as well as a great tool for changing negative stories into positive vibes of self-love and amazeballs. (Yes, that is a word!)

Some say that to receive the maximum benefits from meditation, you should commit to twenty minutes of meditation a day. My experience is that meditating for this amount of time is quite difficult in the beginning. I personally had a hard time focusing!!

Like everything else, meditation takes practice. Some days for me were considerably more difficult than others. I can't tell you the number of times I was in the middle of meditating and instead, ended up cleaning the bathroom sink—and then telling myself off for being so distracted! After a while, though, I would just sit back down and finish meditating. With practice, I gained greater focus and was able to sit with myself for longer.

Many practitioners also recommend meditating at the same time in the same place every day, and preferably in the morning. This prescription didn't work for me either, as my daily schedule is pretty variable. So I just fit it in when and where I can. I even meditate in the car when I am waiting at school pickup! I personally pick the times that are available to me and take it from there.

While eventually you will reach the point where you can meditate in silence, I find prerecorded meditations helpful when just starting out.

Exercise: *Meditate*

Start small–five minutes whenever you get the chance. As stated above, this can even be while you are waiting at school pick up or for the brief moment you escape to your walk in closet.

Search for "free meditations" on Google and start listening to some guided meditations. Even if you just get through the first five minutes, it's a great start.

As there is so much out there, be choosy about the meditations you try: Some may be easier for you than others. Some may resonate with you more than others. Find the ones that are the most inspiring to you.

You also can join meditation groups or classes in most areas, or work one-on-one with coaches or trainers that offer meditations. Once again, the choice is yours.

Yoga

"The yoga pose is not the goal. Becoming flexible is not the goal. Standing on your hands is not the goal.

The goal is to create space where you were once stuck. To unveil the layers of protection you've built around your heart. To appreciate your body and become aware of the mind and the noise it creates. To make peace with who you are. The goal is to love, well... You."
~Rachel Brathen

I love this quote by bestselling author and motivational speaker Rachel Brathen because it demystifies yoga, making it accessible to everyone, and directly speaks to how yoga can benefit the re-discovery of The Amazing You.

You don't need to create that perfect crow pose, because that's not what yoga is about. Yoga is another great mindfulness practice that works with your mind, body and soul and incorporates breathing and meditation. It's a "triple whammy" for relieving stress, increasing your flexibility and strength, and enabling you to access your true, spiritual self. And for us more "creaky" folks (!), yoga is so effective in terms of getting rid of the aches and pains that come with age or injury.

Holistic Healer, Chanelle Fleury pointed out to me that the traditional symbol for yoga is the Lotus flower. Interestingly, the Lotus flower grows in muddy, murky waters to rise and bloom. It symbolically represents being grounded in earth, and reaching for the divine.

The Lotus symbol mirrors the journey that we are all on—not just those of us who have suffered abuse, but anyone who has endured any kind of trauma. And that is most of humanity! We all have trauma we must rise above to become the beautiful flower that we are. According to Fleury, this journey is simply part of the human experience.

There are many types of yoga. I've tried many varieties of yoga, and I like them all for their respective purposes. For example, there is hot yoga, where the room is heated up, which makes your muscles looser and easier to stretch—and also causes you to sweat like a racehorse for a detoxifying effect. There are yoga practices that are more strenuous, such as Vinyasa, and those that are less strenuous and more restorative, such as Yin Yoga.

Exercise: *Yoga*

Different yoga studios have different philosophies—your homework is to go online, visit some studios and do some research. Find one in your area that suits you. It's your choice, remember, and not mine! Many yoga studios will let you attend a class for free and/or have a "first month" offer.

Breathing

Breathing is a big part of most mindfulness practices such as yoga and meditation. When you control your breath, you control mind and body.

I first learned about the importance of breath in Yoga. In Yoga you will notice that each pose is aligned with an inhale or an exhale. This is called Pranayama Breathing. Prana is life force energy. There are a number of other breathing techniques that Yogi's employ to energize the body.

If you are suffering from anxiety and/or PTSD, the simple act of breathing mindfully can help activate your parasympathetic nervous system and bring you back to balance and relaxation. When you breathe, you are bringing life energy (Prana or Chi) to your body. It's a tool for renewal!

As a living example of just how effective breathing can be, Dutch extreme athlete Wim Hof has taken breathing as a tool for healing to the extreme. Wim is noted for his ability to withstand freezing temperatures. He is the world record holder for the longest swim under ice. He crossed the Death Zone in shorts, and fought off a type of bacteria, E. coli, that was directly injected into his bloodstream. How did he achieve all of these seemingly superhuman feats? According to Wim, his secret superpower is breathing.

Wim has proven that through breath, we can control our nervous system to a degree that was never thought possible. It's okay if you don't believe in taking breathing to the level that Wim Hof does: Just taking a deep, slow, breath when you feel you are becoming anxious can work wonders. Try it.

There are many different types of breathing techniques, and a great book for learning them (it also comes with a training CD) is The Healing Power of the Breath: Simple Techniques to Reduce Stress and Anxiety, Enhance Concentration, and Balance Your Emotions, by Richard P. Brown, MD and Patricia L. Gerbarg, MD. It provides an introduction to various breathing techniques, and will more than get you on your way to a more relaxed, integrated life.

In the beginning, focus on those breathing methods that invite relaxation and release as well as cleansing. As you get better at breathing and understanding its direct effects on your nervous system, explore more types. Once again, it's a practice, and in order to get good at it—well, practice makes perfect!!!

Exercise: *Breathe*

Every hour check in and breathe mindfully.

To remind yourself to do this every hour, buy reminder bracelets, download apps (such as Apple's Breathe app) that work on your watch or phone, or simply set your alarm clock. Notice how it makes you feel simply stopping and taking a moment to just breathe.

Visualization

The mindful technique of visualization is key to the creation of this very book: After I visualized, or imagined the ex as a flea, I went on to use this analogy throughout my book to help you begin to see the awful narcissist, sociopath or psychopath in your life for what they are: a small, insignificant, bug.

You might recall that visualization is the technique I used when I got off of the plane and set my feet down on the ground of the scariest place I could have imagined returning to: New Zealand.

Now to many people, New Zealand is a beautiful, peaceful country. But for me, it became the most terrifying place in the world, for it was the place I had to escape from in order to get away from my flea and recover me.

As I first described in Chapter 1, *Discard...*, I had turned the ex into a flea when I got off of the plane, and me into Arwen, the beautiful and empowered warrior riding atop her beautiful horse. I actually used the horse visualization before this, because when I imagine the most powerful, beautiful me, I imagine me riding a horse! Yes, I was that kid who read the horse books, had horse figurines and posters, and begged my parents for riding lessons.

So when you imagine the most powerful you. Who do you imagine? Me, horsewoman. You, who? And before you get all nervous and think this is a total joke. Some of the most famous people you know use this technique. Take Beyonce as an example. Before Beyonce gets on stage she imagines Sasha Fierce. This is her alter ego. The ego that allows her to get on stage and be, well, Beyonce - unbelievable Beyonce. The Beyonce we see anyways. I don't think anyone thinks of Beyonce as anything but fierce. But according to Beyonce herself, she is nothing like her alter ego.

Athletes also use visualization. Have you ever watched ski racers before their race moving and jumping just like they were skiing the course? It looks like the goggles they are wearing are virtual reality glasses as they visualize themselves flying down the hill crushing every obstacle in their way, before they have to do it for real. They are training their brain for success.

I've decided to think of the ex as a flea and use this analogy throughout this book to help you begin to see the awful narcissist, sociopath or psychopath in your life for what they are—a small, insignificant, bug. Start to visualize yourself as something powerful and start to feel your world shift as a result.

So yoga, breathing, visualization and meditation have all been instrumental in my recovery and my quest to retrain my brain. The incredible part is, as you use mindfulness practices, you will change your energy. The bad things around you won't seem as bad. And you will notice (to your surprise) people reacting to you differently.

As you shift your energy, the system around you will change. And yes, even the flea will lose their power over you. The flea will be reduced to exactly what they are, a frickin' flea.

Which leads me to the exercise I have in mind for you...

Exercise: *Visualization*

Visualize the most powerful you. Start to visualize yourself as something powerful–and start to feel your world shift as a result.

Now, when you imagine the most Amazing You, just who do you imagine? You already know that for me, I visualize myself as a horsewoman. But you…who and what are you???

Visualizations are more powerful the more detailed they are, so please, please, please, go nuts! Visualize the most powerful you in in detail. According to Amy Cuddy, Social Psychologist, Author and Speaker, body language changes how we see ourselves–body language changes our energy. According to Cuddy, "power posing"–standing in a posture of confidence can boost feelings of confidence. To get you in the mood, watch her video and mimic the power poses Cuddy recommends.

Video: Your Body Language May Shape Who You Are, Amy Cuddy, Social Psychologist https://www.ted.com/talks/amy_cuddy_your_body_language_may_shape_who_you_are?language=en

Honestly, I can't wait to see what you come up with!!! Share your visualization with me at **project336.co** and I will share some of them with your permission.

Nutrition and exercise

I struggled with whether or not to write about nutrition and exercise specifically. As you can see from previous steps, I engage in exercise regularly. Exercise fills my need to release stress from my body and boost my endorphins, but I also happen to have a very strong community at my local gym. So I get the double whammy of community and health benefits by going to the gym!

I found as I raised my vibration and got out and about more, it was just a natural fit for me to become more aware of my physical body including the amount of exercise I was doing as well as what I was putting into it. After all, I wanted to own Amazing, spiritually, emotionally and physically.

What I found in my discovery process around eating and exercise as well as in my subjective experience is that what you eat also impacts your energy levels. And in fact I found that diet has a much larger impact on your ability to maintain a healthy weight (some say it's 80% of the battle) than exercise alone.

When is comes to exercising, I follow the Matthew McConaughey model of simply doing something every day. For me, I engage in a combination of weight lifting, yoga, biking, walking and high intensity workouts. Some days I fit a 50 minute class in, while other days, I only have time for 30 minutes and a walk with the dogs in the afternoon. I don't keep track, I just schedule in exercise as a calendar event in my diary and I just do it, as I said, almost daily.

What motivates me to exercise is how it makes me feel

as opposed to any specific weight loss goals as well as the camaraderie and friendly competition with my friends at the gym. Although changing the shape of my body has been a welcome, positive side effect! I also can't seem to say "no" to an achievable challenge. I think it has something to do with growing up competing with a twin brother. The question you need to answer for yourself is what motivates you? And what types of exercise do you find enjoyable?

I also try to eat sensibly focusing on the balance of protein, carbohydrates and fats. This is the approach I learned from working with Kenney, who I mentioned is a Sports Nutritionist. Kenney is truly unbelievable in her commitment to eating the right diet and her body shows it. For me, I have found making small adjustments make a huge difference. As one small example, I switched to nut based milk in my morning latte to help me fill my breakfast protein requirement. This was totally simple and an easy choice.

Diet and exercise are personal things so I urge you to find the right balance for you and the right types of exercise. I find if you get exercise by doing the things that you love and eat foods that you like, sticking to daily, exercise and eating right isn't a chore. I do it because it just makes me feel better and brings me closer to The Amazing Me!

Exercise: *Nutrition and exercise*

Talk to a nutritionist about your goals and start small. Even small changes can make a big difference.

Take the exercise challenge and do one small thing daily. This can be a half hour of walking your dog or engaging in a high intensity workout for 30 minutes or committing to 50 lunges a day.

Notice when you feel motivated and when you don't. Do more of the things that you enjoy and less of the things that you don't. For example, I DO NOT LIKE running. (Let's be honest I'd rather swallow a large bug than go for a run.) So guess what, I don't run!

Having more energy motivates me, as well as relieving stress. For me, nutrition was a game changer for energizing my body. What motivates you?

Reminder strategies

"Symbols just remind us of what we already have inside of us." - *Tony Robbins*

Even if you are the most dedicated Yogi around, you can fall into old patterns, replay old stories and react to the next trigger. So first of all, take it easy on yourself. It's been years since my flea left, and I still find myself, on occasion, frantically scratching at the mere mention of the flea. Even when I am in the comfort and security of my own home, panic may get the best of me because the flea won't let me talk to my son, or decides he isn't going to pay for important things like braces, or sends me horrible emails telling me why my son isn't going to be on the next plane to see me. So it's important that you are able to ground yourself with reminder strategies and recognize their patterns of behavior.

I find reminders are very effective for bringing me back to me—for getting back to center and stopping me from falling into old patterns and stories of self-doubt, fear, anxiety, guilt or shame.

For example when you get that terrible email and your nervous system flips into fight or flight mode, you need a way to quickly get back on track. We've talked about several tools already such as breathing and visualization. Reminders are just another tool you can turn to in times of need.

My personal favorite reminders that ground me are…
rocks! Yes, the pretty crystal kind of rocks that emit amazing energy, if you believe in that kind of stuff. And I do: Depending on the day, I choose the crystal that maps to my particular intention and energy requirement, like protection or grounding or self-love. As a general rule of thumb, darker stones are for grounding myself, and they are my favorite

rocks to carry around in my pocket. When I know I'll be engaging in a life-threatening activity, say, going to a party on my own, I simply hold the stone to remind myself that there isn't a proverbial tiger waiting for me on the other side of the door.

I am well aware crystals may not be your thing. You might, for example, love tattoos. Or, your "poison" might be hanging signs around the house stating how awesome you are and how wonderful life is, the necklace you wear around your neck that you can touch or reading your favorite passage in a book.

Yes, your reminders can be anything, simply anything, you love: the smell of your favorite essential oil, an empowering song, a hug from your pet, a picture of your favorite peeps on your desk, or the ring on your finger you just bought yourself to celebrate The Amazing You.

As we work to retrain our brain, we want to train ourselves to feel our emotions, but then move through our fear and negative stories, and as a result, raise our vibration. Reminders empower us to do just that.

Exercise: *Reminder strategies*

Create reminders that are accessible to you and that you can access as frequently as you need to.

For crystal lovers you can visit **project336.co/crystals-protection** and find a list of protective and grounding crystals. Alternatively visit **project336.co/crystals-self-love** and find a list of crystals that will remind you of how amazing you are!

STEP 10

Be wary of lawyers and the legal system

You have to be in the best position you can be for divorcing that flea, fighting that custody battle and achieving the financial security you deserve. The process involves continuing to set boundaries.

Plus, if it's true that we learn from failure, then you need to read this: I am the most learned person around when it comes to how NOT to exit an abusive relationship. Learn from my mistakes!

Here is some of what I learned the hard way…

Get a Lawyer Well Versed in Fleas

Unfortunately, relationships with fleas never end amicably. The flea who just abused you will most likely will leave you in financial ruin, as 99% of fleas abuse their partners financially. Financial abuse is when a person takes financial advantage of another and, as a result, has financial control of that person. This abuse can take the form of controlling assets, keeping a person from working, sabotaging a person's job, assuming debt (created by the flea) and/or a combination of all of the above.

If children are a part of the relationship, this will become complicated once you exit the relationship. You are likely to have some sort of custody battle on your hands. Even if your ex isn't all that interested in the kids, s/he may suddenly "change their tune"–often because they know children provide another avenue to maintain power and control over you!

In both cases, you need a lawyer who understands what fleas are capable of, as well as the impact that the trauma bond has on your ability to make decisions that are in your best interest over the long-term. This bond that you have with the flea leaves you vulnerable to making compromises over money and custody you will regret later in the misguided hope that the flea will do the same for you in return—which they won't.

In the early stages of exiting your relationship, you will be particularly vulnerable to making these very bad judgment calls. The flea will inevitably do something nice (however contrived) and you may think that maybe the flea has some-how "seen the light." They haven't. So your choice of a strong, knowledgeable, experienced lawyer is CRITICAL.

Here are some other important points about dealing with lawyers and the family court system in the hope that you manage to obtain the best possible results for your particular situation.

- **Point #1:** Lawyers Are Not Therapists.
  Do NOT use your lawyer as a therapist. You can put yourself in serious financial debt real quickly as lawyers charge by the minute, and they have HUGE hourly rates. Use your life coach or therapist as your life coach or therapist.

- **Point #2:** Limit Your Reactions to the Flea.
  The flea is going to keep biting to get a reaction from you, so you need to get really smart about

what you really need to respond to (through your lawyer) and what you don't need to respond to. If you are having a hard time with this, find a friend or a coach that has been through huge legal battles themselves. Learn from their mistakes that they share with you. Over time you will become very adept at when you should bring a lawyer in and when you should let things lie. Unless there is a true benefit of responding to that hateful lawyer's letter you just received in the mail, don't do it.

- **Point #3:** Be Realistic in Terms of the Estate. The amount you invest in lawyers to secure your estate and have a custody agreement that works for you should be balanced with an understanding of how large your estate actually is. When you meet with your lawyer, be clear about the amount you are able to invest, and ask them to work within the confines of your budget.

- **Point #4:** There are certain qualities important to look for in your lawyer or lawyers:

  - They have a clear and realistic message for you in terms of the law and what the possible outcomes are, given your situation

  - They don't respond with a letter for every request from the flea. Smart, lawyers that have professional integrity only respond when necessary.

- They have references whom you can contact for a recommendation.

- They are willing to ensure you they will be working on the case when required and will have lower-level staff do the "busy work" at a cheaper rate.

- They understand your financial position, and do not engage you in legal battles that aren't worth the expense, e.g., they clearly explain and balance the risk vs. reward and the potential cost of your divorce proceedings.

Exercise: *Be wary of lawyers and the legal system*

Review Step 4 and the associated exercises in regards to finding the right lawyer that can effectively represent you.

STEP 11

Create boundaries

In order to stop any addiction, you need to stop doing the very thing that you are addicted to. Like an alcoholic going cold turkey, you need to drop the flea completely from your life in order to break the addiction. Stay away from the flea. I repeat, stay away from the flea. This means implementing a regiment of personal, sacred, boundaries and most importantly implement No Contact. By setting boundaries and implementing No Contact, you will gain your power back!

No Contact sets a "mega-boundary" with the flea and is a very important step in enabling you to get on with your life. You see, each time the flea is back in your presence (either physically or via text message, phone call, etc.), it will feel like you just grabbed an electric fence: Your nervous system will be shocked back on high-alert. Re-traumatized by the flea, you will find yourself spiraling back into addiction– back to rock bottom.

Realize when you implement No Contact, you are cutting off all ties with the flea. I repeat, ALL ties. And, according to H.G. Tudor, self-proclaimed narcissist, cutting all ties is what narcissists hate the most!!! You are literally cutting them from their power supply--their narcissistic supply–so why not?? As H.G. Tudor attests, " No Contact [is] the only way to beat the narcissist and achieve freedom."

Get Ready for Tantrums!
When you do begin to create boundaries (such as implementing No Contact) on your own accord and/or through legal agreements, you can expect major tantrums from the flea. Yes, tantrums. Fleas believe they are above the law and will

avoid any boundaries set by you, or the courts, at all costs. (Because they get in the way of them getting access to their supply.) Expect their abusive behavior to continue, and don't underestimate their appetite for cruelty and their ability to manipulate.

And here's another warning: Once you put up the boundaries or establish No Contact, it's very easy to fall into the traps the flea will continue to set to suck you back into their bizarre world. They'll show up at your place of work unannounced just to "say hello," and/or perhaps barrage you with text messages and emails. Don't be shocked when, years later, they might go so far as to drop off old pictures of the two of you or post loving remarks about you on social media, hoping this will cause you to drop your defenses.

Don't Engage
As discussed in Step 10, the flea is going to keep biting to get their narcissistic supply. Keep all communications straight forward and to the point–devoid of emotion–the flea's supply. Even if you have the BEST response or feel the need to share your morality with the flea, remember THEY ARE NOT LISTENING. Once again, your response is falling on deaf ears. Worse, your response is feeding their narcissistic supply and refueling your body with cortisol–keeping your addiction alive.

Trust me. You, in that moment you press send with a brief response devoid of emotion, will instantly gain your power back and free your mind to think about other, way more important things than the flea.

When Kids Are Involved

Some of you out there who have been abused have, like I do, have children from the relationship. So yes, if you have children with the flea and are sharing custody, you will need to communicate about the kids, and this is going to make breaking the addiction harder.

Society puts so much pressure on us to co-parent. But apparently, whomever invented co-parenting never met a flea and their penchant for counter-parenting. And what I mean by counter-parenting is their need to implement the opposite of whatever you would want for your child. So, co-parenting with a flea is a total nightmare, dangerous and extremely destructive to you and potentially to your child(ren). I recommend investigating Parallel Parenting. Parallel Parenting is where you disconnect from the other parent and parent beside them.

So for example, you have your rules in your house, and they have rules in their house. When the flea does something that you don't agree with, work with a therapist that un-derstands fleas to help you talk to your child in a direct and open way about why you don't agree with the flea or the flea's behaviors. This doesn't mean throwing the flea under the bus, it means showing your children an appropriate value system and boundaries.

(We will talk about the importance of detailed, rock solid custody arrangements and parenting communication appli-cations in Step 12.) In either case, whether you can discon-nect from the flea entirely because you don't have children with them, or if you need to Parallel Parent, remember fleas are focused on one thing: filling their need for narcissistic supply. (And I know I keep repeating that point–ON PURPOSE!) It doesn't matter if it's positive attention or negative attention; they will do whatever it takes to get a reaction from you--any reaction.

Parental fleas will set special parenting traps once you set boundaries or establish No Contact. Some examples of their behavior include parking their car next to yours at parenting events and/or standing purposely in your space or surreptitiously filming you with your children and/or making sure you have to walk by them to get to your car at the end of the event and/or dropping unneeded items such as Tupperware or Clothes off at your house with unusual frequency (daily)–all of these antics are done in the name of getting (negative) attention from you.

Upholding No Contact and setting boundaries is very difficult with fleas, but boundaries are critical to your recovery and your children's wellbeing. Don't be hard on yourself if you slip up and engage with the flea. Dig deep, forgive yourself, and look in the mirror and tell yourself you are AMAZING.

No Contact and upholding boundaries takes a lot of practice, but know this: You will–get better at it over time. And over time–sometimes it takes years–the flea will eventually quit biting.

Exercise: *Create boundaries*

Start small and work your way into No Contact. For example, the next email or text you receive from your flea filled with vitriol, respond only to what is absolutely necessary. For example, short responses and directives are best. E.g., "Yes I can or No I cannot. Yes please. No thank you. Please have our daughter call me. Please contact me only through the parenting application."

I can assure you, upon receipt of your brief, emotionless communication, your flea will be shocked. And you will be EMPOWERED.

STEP 12

Highly detailed parenting agreements

If you are one of the few lucky ones, the flea will leave you with your children without making an issue of it. But if s/he sees the kids as another way to control you, and s/he receives narcissistic supply from the kids, s/he will do whatever it takes to maintain control over your children.

Custody is different in every state and country. And as stated before, be very careful about thinking that the courts will recognize your abuser as just that: abusive. Not only is emotional abuse not easily and/or expensive to prove, the courts are ill prepared to deal with abusive situations. Many judges, lawyers and even court-appointed psychologists are not trained to identify and deal with fleas.

Just as they do in their personal relationships, narcissists, psychopaths, covert aggressors and sociopaths will lie and manipulate to get what they want during the legal proceedings. To give you an idea of just how convincing they are, here is my story.

When I first met with my lawyer in 2009, I began a relocation case to take my son back to the USA. I truly believed justice would be served. The flea would be exposed. So I had set my heart on going home with my son. After all, I was going to go through the system, and I was going to win because I was the victim. Justice would be done. Right? Wrong.

Information-gathering for the relocation case was incredibly time consuming and financially draining. During this time the lawyers wrote devastating letter after devastating letter back and forth, back and forth, accusing the other party of misbehavior, rogue text messages, emails and the like, basically all in the name of case-building.

A psychological review conducted by a court-appointed psychologist was also required for the relocation case. When we first met, I told the psychologist that my ex was emotionally abusive and that he would physically threaten me. Then I then talked about my son, his sensitive nature, and how he deserved better. I explained what I felt the US had to offer him, and how much better our quality of life would be on the same income. I also asked the psychologist to look at our financials so she could see in the details of the financial abuse I had endured, and to what extent the ex was capable of lying and manipulating. I felt she needed to know he was not a sound role model.

The psychologist then told me our financials were not part of her brief, and were irrelevant. So that part was bad—and things got worse. The psychologist repeatedly asked me inappropriate and irrelevant questions. She wanted me to paint a detailed picture for her as to when my son walked and said his first word. I tried to recount those events as best I could, but at one point she flew into a rage yelling at me, "You don't remember, do you?" The psychologist also asked me repeatedly about the fact that I had experienced postpartum depression. She wanted to know "how bad" it was, and she demanded the details over and over again.

When her report about the ex and I came out, it noted, among other things, that I was "neurotic," "emotional" and a deluded American. As for the flea, with whom she had also met, his lies were throughout the report–apparently she had believed everything he had said about me and our life together, even though it ended up making her very own report contradictory.

His inconsistencies and contradictions were rampant in her report. For example, on the one hand I was "obsessed" with my infant son and "would not leave him with anyone, or let anyone touch him," while on the hand I was a "negligent," " ambivalent" mother who went off horseback riding or getting her hair done for hours on end while I left my son with my mother-in-law. How could I be both? Negligent in terms of my son, and yet so obsessive about with my son that I wouldn't ever leave him in another's care?

The flea's lies were perceived to be the truth by the psychologist, no matter how far-fetched they were or how they could be contradicted by his previous statements or proof, such as proof available to her in our financial documents that she ignored. According to the psychologist, I was "deluded" in my perceptions of my husband.
In short the ex won, and I came out the crazy one! Based on that result, I didn't even proceed with the relocation (of my son with me to the U.S.) case: My lawyer advised me that I simply could not win, based on that report.

The important point I'm trying to make here is: Once you put your fate in the hands of a professional untrained in spotting fleas, anything can happen. So be very, very careful. If it's possible, demand that the Court Appointed Psychologist has experience with narcissist, psychopaths, sociopaths and emotional abuse. If not, you really are rolling the dice.

Establishing a Parenting Agreement
Ensure the parenting agreement ultimately settled upon is very, very detailed. As painful as it is to read, read it. Know it inside and out. Then stick to it. You will find that fleas will try to create their own rules, their own reality, which is why having a highly detailed parenting agreement is *crucial*.

In my experience (and as discussed earlier), fleas have ever changing and extremely poor boundaries, which they redefine like the wind to suit their needs. The flea will want to stay in control of you and/or the kids in any way they can. Some examples include, frequent changing of parenting days, arriving late for pick-ups and drop-offs, or not showing up at all. They may tell you that they "absolutely" have to attend something with the kids on your parenting day, as well as control when the children can or cannot talk to you. Don't be surprised when they make up their own reality, such as telling you there are eight days in one week instead of seven or the sky is not blue, it's green. I'm not kidding; this happens!

When you say "no" to any of their requests or behaviors, they will blame you for being "inflexible" and/or tell you are a "bad" mom or dad. Ignore them. Simply remind the flea they are "....bound by a court-enforced agreement to do X, Y and Z." I find copying and pasting the exact wording from the agreement into emails and texts is very helpful in stopping the back-and-forth and ensuring the flea sticks to the rules.

Another recommendation is finding a parenting application of your choice that will keep a record of all interactions between you and the flea and build this into any parenting arrangement if you have children with the flea.

Parenting applications such as Taking Parents as one example do three things.

1. They give you a central place where all of your communications with the flea are recorded.

2. Since communications are recorded, it will help you stay accountable to you for keeping communications between the two of you simple, to the point, devoid of emotion, and focused on the kids.

3. Having the application limits the number of communications tools the flea can use to harass you.

The boundaries that are set in the parenting agreement and the use of the parenting application will be a godsend as you maneuver your way through parallel parenting with a flea.

STEP 13

Get your financial house in order

Abusers use finances as another way to control their victims. As stated earlier, if someone is abusing you, there is a 99% chance they are abusing you financially, and unless you are among the lucky 1%, you've got a big, big problem on your hands. NOW, immediately, is the time to get your finances in order, because the chances that you are among the 1% who aren't or won't be in trouble, is, well, 1%.

Hold onto this thought. Digest it deeply. The black and white nature of most financial activities can be instrumental in breaking the trauma bond and helping you to accept the fact that the love of your life is a flea. For example, if your partner has been racking up debt in your name and/or draining your accounts, there is factual data in the form of account statements that can be easily collected and analyzed. This black and white data will be hard for you to deny–yes they abused you.

Money is Not a Dirty Word
You must have money in order to survive, let alone hire the professional help you need–especially if you need to fight for your money or engage in a custody battle for your children.

When my ex left, the lawyers I talked to said, "Don't worry about the money, worry about your son first. If you go after the money, the courts will think you are money-hungry."

Well, that is the STUPIDEST (and most sexist) piece of advice on the planet earth.

You see, without money, you can't fight for what is rightfully yours. And if you have kids, the legal battle with the flea will most likely continue until your children are fully grown and making decisions on their own. Bottom line. And remember this. It is your money. IT IS YOUR MONEY.

Money is Independence

In my experience, if you aren't smart about your finances, the flea will win and you will end up with nothing. I know this because I did: My flea controlled everything, and he took 85% of our wealth - 85% of which I earned. Again, please learn from my mistakes. You must treat your finances as just that: finances—as you would in a business.

To give you an idea of just how focused on winning fleas are, I will share a bit of my financial story. Once you read this you will know that if they can ensure you end up on your ass in the middle of the desert with only the clothes on your back, or maybe no clothes - they will.

The flea would always tell me that I "didn't understand money." This was the reason why, he said, I didn't need to attend meetings with the accountants or lawyers in regard to our properties. And he was right, I didn't understand money. Certainly not in the way he and my brother-in-law did. Besides, he loved me, didn't he? He wouldn't do anything to hurt me. So I trusted his judgment.

Early in our relationship, the flea set up a meeting with me, his brother-in-law, and his brother-in-law's lawyer to set up a family trust. Together they convinced me that my flea was doing me a great favor by setting up the trust and letting us borrow money from it for our family home. At the time, I really didn't understand why we needed to borrow money from the trust as I had just paid for our holiday house and was making more than enough money to pay the mortgage. However, I trusted the three of them and that they were creating the right financial structure for our family. The flea and I were planning to create a nest egg by investing in property. He would use his business connections to renovate the properties and/or build them, and I would work to fund the renovations and investments.

Being from the USA, I had no idea about how trusts operated in New Zealand. But in short, they are a financial tax haven for the rich as well as a way the rich protect their assets. Once your property is in the trust, only the trustees can make decisions regarding the trust.

While we were married, the flea put the properties that we were building and / or renovating into the trust. The whole time, I never saw an accountant or a lawyer or a bank manager. This was his domain. How stupid was I? Especially since he was using my income to borrow money for our properties.

It wasn't until years later, when a friend of ours—an accountant—called me into his office, that I was made aware that something was very, very wrong. The ex had temporarily handed our accounts over to this friend of ours to manage (to this day I'm not sure why).

Our friend sat me down and proceeded to tell me that he didn't like what the flea and my brother-in-law were doing to me. I asked him what he meant.

He explained to me with a simple drawing that I was only a beneficiary of the family trust—which meant basically I didn't own or have any say in the properties I invested in, the Flea and his brother-in-law did. Further, because of the way the trust was structured, should the ex and I get divorced, I would end up with—nothing. The structure they had set up ensured the ex and my brother-in-law could one day walk away with everything, leaving me destitute.

In short, the flea had put all of our money and rental properties under a trust in his and my brother-in-law's name. Plus, we had borrowed money from the trust to buy our family home—so when we sold it the trust that would get repaid, not me! I effectively had invested all of my earnings in a company I owned none of, and had no control over.

The flea now lives in a million dollar house with five rental properties paying for his retirement. As you can imagine, the bank owns most of my one condo.

So, what is the moral of the story? Make sure you understand your complete financial picture as fast as you can.

Make all decisions consciously, and become fully informed. Without the money to fortify yourself against these bastards, you are toast.

The Justice System is Not Like In the Movies

As you can see from my experience, the justice system is NOT like in the movies. It's very easy to lose control of your future when you put it in the hands of professionals that don't understand how to deal with fleas.

In real life, lawyers are there to understand the law and provide you with the best advice they can regarding what you can achieve within the confines of the law. Unfortunately, in my experience at least, the law has little to absolutely nothing to do with justice. It's a hard pill to swallow—but grab that glass of water and swallow it. Now it's time to move on and manage it as best as you can.

Exercise: *Get your financial house in order*

Visit **project336.com** to download a financial worksheet that will help you get a handle on your assets and liabilities.

Here are some other tips for understanding your financial picture:

- Collect the mail for a month and from that, create a spreadsheet of all of your assets and liabilities using the worksheet provided.

- Check to see if your flea has sold any cars or large assets recently and not subsequently deposited the money into your joint accounts and/or made any large purchases such as a new car.

- Create a spreadsheet of all of the money going in and out of your bank accounts over the past five years, how much each of you contributed, and where the money went.

- Create a spreadsheet of all of your credit cards. How much is owed and who's name the credit cards are in.

- Search the house for hidden amounts of cash, including the attic, stairwells, garage, etc.

STEP 14

Create your vision

"The silver lining to your healing journey is that it led you to the path of the Great Work, the alchemy of Spirit by which we turn the lead of the psyche to radiant gold and become all we can be, all that we are destined to be-illuminated beings of limitless potential."
Creative Alchemy: The Science of Miracles,
Stephanie Sinclaire Lightsmith

I recently found a book I used to read to my son when he was little called, You Choose, by Pippa Goodhart and Nick Shrratt. It was his favorite. On each page my son could choose from images of the most interesting house to live in, the craziest hat he wanted to wear or his perfect form of transportation. A spaceship? Sure. A race car? Absolutely. A riverboat? No problem. He could choose. And it struck me recently as I opened the book again for the millionth time, giggling at the images and remembering my son's little sticky finger pointing as we moved from picture to picture, how profound this book really is: All of us have the ability to choose. We can not only choose how we live or what hat we wear, but what kind of partner we want as well as how we react to any situation. We also can choose our belief system, or our values. It's up to us.

And yet somehow, through my need for certainty and love, I had done a deal with the devil himself. For years, I choose certainty in exchange for my soul, my integrity and my ability to choose the life I dreamed of.

Awakening to your inner warrior and refinding The Amazing You is realizing you have a choice. Life isn't happening to you; YOU happen to life. You choose the stories you accept as your own, not the flea. Emotions aren't happening to you; YOU choose your emotional state. It's your job to use this amazing gift called life and choose to live it in a way that aligns with who you are. You choose to live it in a way that aligns with your integrity.

And now that you have chosen to walk away from addiction

and a terrible kind of love, and a flea, you get to choose. So what is your vision for the life you choose? It's time to create it.

Vision is about designing YOUR future. It's about manifesting what you want. It's about using the tools we have discussed in this book to decide where you want to be and what you want your life to look like. Don't worry about the steps to get there: Once you create your vision you will begin to notice things and attract experiences that align with your vision, with what you choose for yourself.

For example, I created a vision of the man I wanted to be with; it came complete with a list of emotional attributes, eating habits and a love of the outdoors. I also created a vision for the energy I wanted in my home, and how I wanted to feel each and every time I walked in its door. PEACEFUL, pretty much summed up that one!

You too can create multiple visions. Your vision might include getting a veterinarian degree, starting your own restaurant, or choosing an intention such as peace or love. Whatever it is, creating it starts with your imagination and leaving judgment behind.

Write your vision down and adjust it as you gather more information and gain a deeper connection with who you are.

Manifesting
Creating a vision will change your energy and begin to shift the world around. You will notice the universe (or whatever

that is for you) introducing you to the things that will help you manifest the life you desire and deserve. The life you choose. This vision is the foundation for manifesting what you want.

First you have ask yourself the question.

What do you want? What does Amazing mean to you? Then, write it down.

Then with your vision in hand, think about it, meditate on it, yoga on it, breathe on it! What you think, is that you become and what you attract from the world around you (remember the Law of Attraction?). Managing your thoughts are the key to manifesting your future. What are you thinking about in this moment? By letting go of old stories you will find you now have time to focus on positive thoughts of The Amazing You.

Having a vision is also a useful tool for keeping you on track and in alignment with your integrity. For example, if you have a vision for achieving a life of peace (definitely part of my vision!), the decision to let go of any person, place or thing that doesn't align with your vision of peace becomes clear. As you approach the world in a peaceful state, the people and the world around you will begin to relate to you differently. Take notice. This is a really exciting time in your journey back to you, as you assume even greater control of your existence and experience your vision manifesting itself in the most unexpected of ways.

Exercise: *Create your vision*

Create your vision or create several.

Go to **project336.co** to download the vision meditation. Now, meditate on your vision for six weeks.

Your vision can be a vision for your future, a thing you desire, or an intention such as self-love. (Maybe for something as simple as driving in the snow without fear!) Notice how your thoughts begin to manifest themselves in reality in the most surprising of ways.

STEP 15

Dating

At some point, you will want to begin dating again too. I know, because I did. But I did it with support. You see, when I first joined a dating site after being rid of my flea, I was working with a psychologist whom I trusted. So I let her know that I was going to start online dating, but that I would report back to her each week about the dates. I wanted her to be my sounding board. If some guy sounded like a jerk, I wanted her to say so.

I would go on a date, and then to my date's unknown horror I would recount my experience back to my psychologist during my next session.

"So there was this guy…"

After all, she was there to keep me on track and away from the fleas. And as I spoke about my dates, sometimes she would bark, "Narcissist!" "Asshole!" "Disordered!"

At first I would fight back with the usual retort, make excuses for any untoward behavior and focus on what they did well. "But wasn't it nice that he…" "And it was really nice when he…" "And I think you are wrong, for even though he did that bad thing, he has a really nice side..." (Sound familiar?!)

Well, she would bark once again, "Narcissist!" and we would laugh out loud. Sometimes we would be in tears we were laughing so hard.

But the serious side of it all was that I knew I needed to

reset my dating compass, and she was there to tell me the truth. Engaging in this exercise with her helped me to reset my expectations in terms of what "normal" looks like and what was abnormal.

For example, I was so used to being treated so badly that I would find myself watching in quiet disbelief as my date went up to the bar to buy me a drink. "A drink? Sure." Like he was buying me the Hope Diamond or something. And it was fun. It was fun to be reminded that there are nice people in the world and like a person that had just traversed the Mohave Desert of kindness and chivalry for the previous countless years—it was nice to be treated, well, like I deserved to be treated. And overtime I began to think, "Oh yeah. I REMEMBER. I AM TOTALLY WORTH IT."

Just between you and me, I still experience this "oh my gosh why are you are being nice to me?" Feeling on occasion. But I've come to the conclusion (over much hard work and many hours of good and bad dates) that I am pretty amazing. The "oh my gosh" feeling has dissipated over time, but kindness still has the ability to catch me off guard.

Dating helped me complete a MUCH NEEDED full reset on my expectations. Dating with the support of a psychologist helped me to avoid falling into the abuse trap again—the type of relationship with which I had become oh-so-familiar.

And that's the thing: I was so used to being abused that it was hard for me to gauge how someone is really supposed to treat you—even on a simple date.

During this time I went on dates with different types of men. I got taken to some great places and events like football games and amazing dinners. [(And you too will be shocked and amazed when you do go out with a nice, normal person. (Did he just offer to get my drink? Huh? :-)] Some turned out to be nice guys. Others, I would never give the time of day to now. Not because I was too good for them, but because they were not nice people. They were narcissists, sociopaths and the like. I had had ENOUGH of those kinds!!

Exercise: *Dating*

Go ahead and make a list of what your ideal partner looks like. It's really important as you date to have a clear idea of what you want in your ideal significant other.

The description can change over time as you gather more information. But if you engage in the "consulting" dating strategy with a mentor, coach or psychologist like I did, share your vision description with them so they have something against which to gauge your discussions.

Keep the traits of your ideal mate close to your heart, and don't deviate from your must-haves. This will help you stop making excuses as you date. Relax and have fun. You deserve it.

Now, go ahead and start!

Own Amazing!

"To realize one's destiny is a person's only obligation."
The Alchemist, Paulo Coelho

Awakening happens by mustering up the courage to take small steps. Little wins will empower you to take bigger more adventurous leaps into your amazing future. Order that bottle of wine that you like at dinner, take that hike, drive your car where you would have never driven before, go to that dinner party that you would have shied away from in the past, try something adventurous like surfing, hiking or mountain biking, and/or join the gym and make it simply a part of your daily routine.

NOW is the time to adopt the just do it mentality.

These activities, although simple, can seem terrifying at first, but when you accept the fear, move through it, and then end up on the other side you will realize you are totally capable - capable of anything you desire or choose to become.

If you have a hard time taking the first step, find a friend, psychologist, coach or mentor, and lean on them. People will feel your energy has shifted and respond to your request for help in the best, most unexpected ways.

As you feel more and more empowered, you will let go of the flea and their legacy a little at a time. This letting go opens up a whole new world of possibilities and empowers you to take advantage of them. Letting go, implementing boundaries and forgiving yourself means freeing up your brain space to focus on your vision for the future. A future in which the flea has no part. It's your vision.

And then, one day, if the flea sends you another horrible

email, text or lawyer's letter, you will feel nothing. Absolutely nothing. And that is the moment you know you are truly flea-free and living a life that is bug-free.

Epilogue

Changing the way the world views emotional abuse

Laws around emotional abuse need to change. In order
to accomplish this, we need to change the perception and
language around emotional abuse. The only thing covert
about emotional abuse is that the victim loses themselves in
the perpetrator's games. This is no different than in physical
abuse: Abuse is abuse. Although emotional abuse may be
hard for the victim to identify, it's obvious to an outsider
who is trained at spotting fleas. Abuse and its effects tend
to be well documented. Evidence of abuse can be found in
texts, emails, financial documents and activities, voicemail
messages and incessant calls, and so on. Emotional abuse
includes physical intimidation and can often escalate to
physical abuse. Again, abuse is multi-layered.

Holding perpetrators of emotional abuse accountable is
beginning to happen around the world. As part of the country's Domestic Violence Act 2018, Ireland now recognizes
"coercive control" as domestic violence, and it is punish-
able by up to five years in prison. How does the Act define
coercive control? As: "...psychological abuse in an intimate
relationship that causes fear of violence, or serious alarm or
distress that has a substantial adverse impact on a person's
day-to-day activities."

Ultimately we need to work together to change the dialog
and remove any stigma associated with emotional abuse. As
well as make litigation more accessible so no other human

on the planet has to suffer at the hands of an abuser.

Education is critical–especially the education of profession-als working in the court system and supporting victims. Professionals working in family court need to understand how to identify narcissists, psychopaths, covert aggressors and sociopaths. These perpetrators are charming. No doubt. On the flip-side, victims are often still caught in the trauma bond and are unable to disconnect themselves from abusive control and will defend their flea.

While I was claiming abuse, not only did the professionals in the New Zealand court system ignore my claim, worse, I was forced to meet with my abuser twice a week. Such court-ordered meetings are simply unacceptable. In addi-tion, as 99% of abusers abuse their victims financially, the state of the finances should be considered alongside any psychological evaluation and should be a huge red flag to anyone working in family court situations and/or in any court proceeding. A claim of abuse needs to be taken seri-ously. And in abusive situations, Court Ordered Parenting Agreements in New Zealand (and other countries) need to be in place beyond the age of 16 years of age.

Financial and legal education is also critical. For exam-ple, I had no idea what a trust was when I moved to New Zealand, and it wasn't until I was in the throes of divorce that I scrambled to understand my financial position and my rights regarding moving back home to the States with my son. How many people know their legal rights and obligations in marriage and divorce? How about in overseas marriages? Only a very small percentage in both cases, leaving people involved in abusive relationships particularly vulnerable.

In the case of international marriages, implementing pre-nuptial agreements that go beyond spelling out the terms of the division of assets should the marriage fail is another missed opportunity. These agreements can facilitate helpful conversations between couples and document the terms of their relationship. Do you want kids? If so, should we get divorced, which country will the children be brought up in? It would have been extremely helpful if the ex and I had spelled out in a such a document our agreement as to what country our children would live in should our marriage fail.

When there is greater legal and documented clarity before a commitment, couples may have a better chance at a success-ful marriage or relationship. For people who inadvertently become involved with a narcissist, sociopath or psychopath, this documentation can be a critical piece of evidence in the courts.

In short, we aren't doing enough to protect victims of emo-tional abuse.

-Elyssa Nager, November 2019

Resources

Amen, Daniel G., M.D., Change Your Brain, Change Your Life: The Breakthrough Program for Conquering Anxiety, Depression, Obsessiveness, Lack of Focus, Anger and Memory Problems. Revised and expanded edition. New York: Harmony Books, 2015.

Brown MD, Richard P., Gerbarg MD, Patricia L., The Healing Power of the Breath: Simple Techniques to Reduce Stress and Anxiety, Enhance Concentration and Balance Your Emotions, Shambhala, 2012.

Canfield, Jack, Life Lessons For Mastering the Law of Attraction: Chicken Soup for the Soul. Westland, 2008.

Chödrön, Pema, Start Where You Are: A Guide to Compassionate Living. Boston: Shambhala Classics, 2001.

Klein, Joey, The Inner Matrix: A Guide to Transforming Your Life and Awakening Your Spirit. 2014.

Lightsmith, Stephanie Sinclaire, Creative Alchemy: the Science of Miracles: create the life you were born to live, co-create a better world. Creative Alchemy Publishing, 2020.

MacKenzie, Jackson, Psychopath Free: Recovering from Emotionally Abusive Relationships with Narcissists, Sociopaths and Other Toxic People. New York: Berkley Books, 2015.

Miller, Meredith, The Journey: A Roadmap to Self-healing After Narcissistic Abuse. 2017.

Morningstar, Dana, Out of the Fog: Moving from Confusion to Clarity After Narcissistic Abuse. Morningstar Media, 2017.

National Intimate Partner and Sexual Violence Survey, 2015 Data.

Brief - Update Release, National Center for Injury Prevention and Control of the Centers for Disease Control and Prevention.

Payson M.S.W, Elenor D., The Wizard of Oz and other Narcissists: Coping with the One-Way Relationship in Work, Love and Family, Julian Day Publications, 2009.

Simon Ph.D., Dr. George K., In Sheep's Clothing: Understanding and Dealing with Manipulative People. Parkhurst Brothers Publishers Inc., 2010.

Stahl Ph.D., Philip, Parenting After Divorce: Resolving Conflicts and Meeting Your Children's Needs. Rebuilding Books, 2007.

Tarrant, Jeff PhD, BCN, Meditation Interventions to Rewire the Brain: Integrating Neuroscience Strategies for ADHD, Anxiety, Depression & PTSD, PESI Publishing and Media, 2017.

Tudor, H.G., No Contact: The Only Way to Beat the Narcissist And Achieve Freedom. Insight Books, 2016.

Tudor, H.G., Sitting Target: How and Why the Narcissist Chooses You. Insight Books, 2016.

Wambach, Abby, Wolfpack: How to Come Together, Unleash Our Power and Change the Game. New York: Celadon Books, 2019.

Made in the USA
Coppell, TX
04 June 2020